MONTROSE

MONTROSE

life in a garden

Nancy Goodwin

with illustrations by Ippy Patterson

FOREWORD BY MAUREEN QUILLIGAN

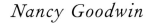

Duke University Press

Durham & London

2005

© 2005 Duke University Press

Illustrations © 2005 Ippy Patterson

All rights reserved

Printed in the United Kingdom on acid-

free paper ∞ by Butler & Tanner, Ltd.

Designed by C. H. Westmoreland

Typeset in Monotype Fournier with

Octavian display by Tseng Information

Systems, Inc.

Library of Congress Cataloging-in-

Publication Data appear on the last

printed page of this book.

Duke University Press gratefully

acknowledges the support of the Mary

Duke Biddle Foundation, which provided

funds for the production and distribution

of this book.

frontispiece: *Cyclamen hederifolium*

TO MONTROSE

PAST, PRESENT, AND FUTURE

CONTENTS

FOREWORD

When my husband Michael Malone and I first came househunting in Hillsborough, North Carolina, I was interested in the town very specifically because I knew there was a famous garden there—Nancy Goodwin's Montrose. That we subsequently bought the property adjoining Montrose was a source of joy to me, for gardens are among the great pleasures of my life. The day we moved into Burnside, our new home, I went to the phone book to look up the number of Montrose. The number wasn't there. Nancy Goodwin had closed the nursery that I had been hoping to use to stock my own new garden. Sadly ready to make do with other sources, I was driving off to purchase plants one morning when I passed a small sign on a brick pillar.

M-O-N-T-R-O-S-E

Craning my neck as I drove along the walled road past the entrance, I felt a little like Satan in Milton's *Paradise Lost*. I was looking in on Paradise, but was able to see only the tops of delicious trees and the sides of the verdant slopes. Worse, unlike Satan, I could not, however willing to do so, "oerleap all bound." Montrose was an Eden and I was outside it.

As it happened, because Hillsborough is a town of many extraordinary artists, like Ippy Patterson, like Nancy Goodwin herself, a month later I found myself invited to tour the gardens at Montrose. Learning of my interest, novelist Allan Gurganus asked Michael and me over for drinks to meet Nancy and Craufurd Goodwin. The evening was a wonderful occasion, and although we later went to dinner at a fashionable restaurant where nobody could hear anyone else, we struck up a rapport, and have happily become over the years good friends as well as neighbors. Shortly after our meeting, I made my first visit to Montrose. It was the beginning of an amazing education.

When I asked Nancy how she designed her garden, she answered, "on my knees." That is the same way her fellow artist and friend Ippy Patterson drew the illustrations for this book. All garden books give readers very different advice—that you should start, not by planting "on your knees," but with a plan on graph paper. Earlier I had helped to design a border in Connecticut in just this way. At first I didn't know what Nancy meant by her remark. But now I think I do. Her artistry begins in an incredible specificity, at the scale of the fingernail on her little finger, the nail she once used to show me a tiny cyclamen, lifting up the leaves carefully one by one, pointing out the way the stems curled on themselves before they unfurled. I had never before paid attention in that way to life so small and so wonderfully perfect.

As has been notoriously remarked, there was never a fully charted overview of the garden at Montrose—not until the map drawn for this book. It is telling and deliberate that tours of the Montrose garden did not offer such a map. In Nancy's view, there can be no substitute for the direct experience of walking the garden step by physical step, moment by particular moment, through time. As a result, we see the garden as Nancy planted it, seed by seed, without any abstract graph imposed upon our direct and immediate experience of individual plants in all their singularity and amazing juxtapositions. The details of Montrose are as precise as any caesura in Milton's poetry, and just as Milton claimed to write by letting the "Heavenly Muse" speak through him, so Nancy claims to let the plants plant themselves.

I trust it is clear that, as a scholar of the arts, I take gardening as seriously as painting or poetry. Gardening—the way Nancy practices it—is, moreover, an art that requires not only great talent but enormous discipline and knowledge, memory and skill, as well as sustained arduous labor. Nancy is so willing and able a teacher that one forgets, sometimes, at what a terrific remove she is from the ordinary garden hobbyist. Whether she is standing in freezing cold demonstrating to a class how to untangle with discarded dental tools the tiny roots of seedlings, or is speaking through a megaphone to a large troop of garden tourists, she is so unpretentious and accessible that one can forget just how august her mastery of her art is.

Some time ago, I asked casually why she happened to be going to the Philadelphia Flower Show—an annual event I had never missed while I lived in Philadelphia, especially because the judges' remarks—often posted next to each exhibit—were such enjoyable studies in acerbic critique. When she responded, "I go to judge it," noting that she'd done so before, I thought, "Of course!" It was delightful to imagine a few of the Main Line matrons I had met years earlier, trembling before the knowledge and the style that Nancy would bring to her analysis of their offerings. For Nancy is as brilliant a writer as she is a gardener. She is able to create, in the words of a paragraph, portraits of experience that are as particular and as intense as the flowers she plants. Two artists created this book together. The drawings of Ippy Patterson both illustrate Nancy's garden and illuminate Nancy's prose. I first encountered Ippy's literally eye-catching talent while dining in a restaurant where strong and beautiful line drawings filled the walls. Throughout the evening I was unable to stop staring at these pictures—although seldom do I notice art in restaurants at all, except, usually, to regret that they are there. Subsequently, as tends to happen in Hillsborough, I had the good fortune to meet Ippy at an elegant private home where there was prominently displayed a drawing by her of the seven deadly sins. Ippy's finely detailed sins were so witty, grotesque, and compelling that again I found myself unable to stop looking at the work, even in the midst of a social bustle. It was a surprise to learn that these intricate knotted tangles of wittily sinful chaos had been drawn by the same artist whose sweeping line had etched out the smooth, innocently naked figures on the restaurant walls. What is always striking about Ippy's art is her control of line at any scale. In this gift, she is very much like Nancy, who works in such various dimensions, from single miniscule plants to alleys of large trees. Ippy has mastered the enigmas of the tiniest botanical detail. It is a perfect mirror of Nancy's small-scale miracles. Similarly, just as Montrose is, as a whole, a dazzling unity, so Ippy's work reflects her understanding of interlaced structure across vast interlinking segments. It is seeing the whole that allows her to be able to see the details so well. Nancy, who is also an accomplished pianist, told me once that she wanted to play the Goldberg Variations on her harpsichord before she died. To me that comment made her "perfect" as an artist. She is someone who has never stopped trying to make all parts of her life into art. Ippy shares that kind of perfection; her gift is visible in her own beauty, in her home, in her contributions to her community, artistic, social, and civic, just as it is present in her paintings and drawings. For both Ippy and Nancy, even as their art constantly changes and evolves, it is at every moment full and complete and present to them. Montrose, the place you will come to know through Nancy's words and Ippy's drawings, is not only home to the exquisite flora that makes it a world-class garden; it is also a house, and a home. The elegant house itself is historic, important to the heritage of North Carolina. The Goodwins have filled its rooms with important collections of domestic art and antiques: coverlets, brass candlesticks, and a large assemblage of Bloomsbury art. It is significant that, in addition to paintings by such artists as Duncan Grant, Roger Fry, and Vanessa Bell, the Goodwin collection includes domestic artifacts often not thought of as high art — painted shutters, tiles from Virginia Woolf's garden table, dinnerware and crockery of all types (hand-painted cups, bowls, plates, and dishes). These pieces have their home in the kind of domestic interior spaces in which Bloomsbury art was meant to be used and seen. At Montrose, art is both lived and lived in. The preservation of all great artistic works, of course, depends upon the nurture of subsequent generations. But the garden is a form of art particularly susceptible to the ravages of time, and for a garden to be uncared for by even one generation risks its loss. Having been selected as a preservation project of the Garden Conservancy, Montrose is poised to have its posterity preserved both as garden and as a house museum. But beyond that, this book is itself not only a work of art but also a means of preserving another work of art, the garden of Montrose. Together Nancy Goodwin's words and Ippy Patterson's illustrations serve to stave off time by taking us in precise, elegant detail through time, by offering us crisp, wise testimony to what a year at Montrose feels like as it passes. Montrose is located in "Historic Hillsborough," the eighteenth-century capital of Orange County, North Carolina. That the town retains many of its beautiful eighteenth- and nineteenth-century houses is due in part to the efforts of William Alexander Graham, former governor of North Carolina and owner of Montrose. Today Hillsborough is (like Concord, Massachusetts, long ago) a small town where a large number of prominent artists—novelists, poets, essayists, painters, musicians, and workers in crafts—make a home and a community. It is a town in which Nancy may appear on a Friday night as the maid in an amateur play production for which Ippy has painted the sets, and then on Saturday afternoon be welcoming hundreds of visitors to Open Day at Montrose, while in her own home Ippy is hosting a gathering of eminent scientists. The lives of both these women are filled with the activities of art. One evening, seated in the midst of a dinner conversation among fellow Hillsborough artists, Nancy remarked, "I hope this never ends." On the pages of the beautiful book that Ippy and she have created together, the year at Montrose passes by us in all the transient particularities of its seasonal changes. But Montrose as a work of art never ends.

MAUREEN QUILLIGAN

ACKNOWLEDGMENTS

Cathy Dykes and Cheryl Traylor work without complaint to maintain the garden. Their skill, knowledge, and energy give me the time to record our activities and write about the joy of living with other creatures in a garden. Joanne Ferguson, Allan Gurganus, Maureen Quilligan, Reynolds Smith, and Daisy Thorp read the manuscript and made perceptive suggestions, which we followed. Malcolm Grear showed us how art and text could flow together and form an integrated work. Neil Patterson and Craufurd Goodwin encouraged us and gave us the constructive criticisms that led us in the right direction. Without any of these friends this book would not be possible. Ippy and I are enormously grateful.

I have attempted to verify the botanical names as they exist in 2004. Botanical taxonomy and nomenclature are under constant revision and some of the current names may have changed by the time this book is published. My primary reference is the *RHS Plant Finder 2004–2005*. When a plant is not listed there, I consult encyclopedias and botanical floras, primarily *The New York Botanical Garden Illustrated Encyclopedia of Horticulture*, *The New Royal Horticultural Society Dictionary of Gardening*, and *Manual of the Vascular Flora of the Carolinas*.

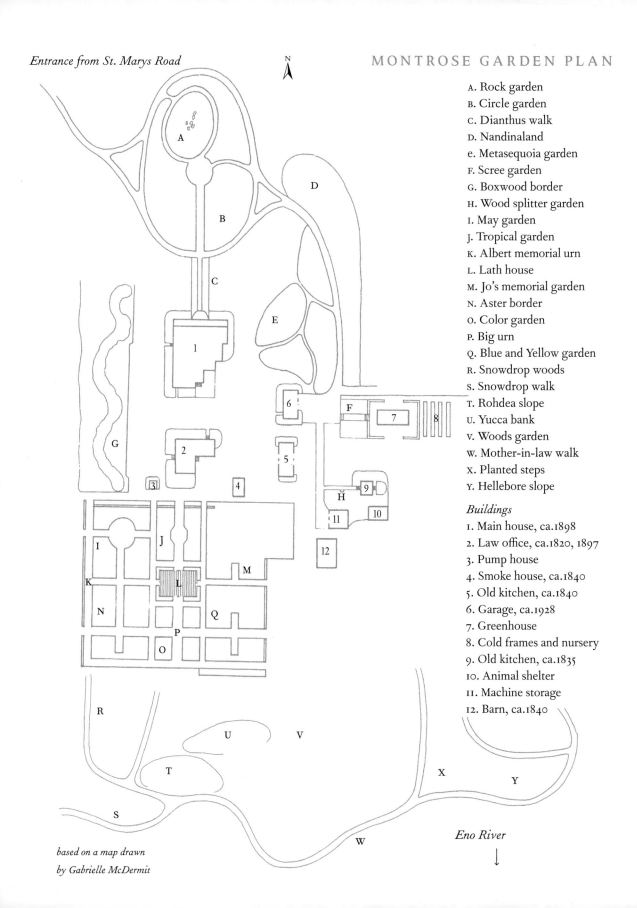

Entrance from St. Marys Road

N

MONTROSE GARDEN PLAN

A. Rock garden
B. Circle garden
C. Dianthus walk
D. Nandinaland
e. Metasequoia garden
F. Scree garden
G. Boxwood border
H. Wood splitter garden
I. May garden
J. Tropical garden
K. Albert memorial urn
L. Lath house
M. Jo's memorial garden
N. Aster border
O. Color garden
P. Big urn
Q. Blue and Yellow garden
R. Snowdrop woods
S. Snowdrop walk
T. Rohdea slope
U. Yucca bank
V. Woods garden
W. Mother-in-law walk
X. Planted steps
Y. Hellebore slope

Buildings
1. Main house, ca.1898
2. Law office, ca.1820, 1897
3. Pump house
4. Smoke house, ca.1840
5. Old kitchen, ca.1840
6. Garage, ca.1928
7. Greenhouse
8. Cold frames and nursery
9. Old kitchen, ca.1835
10. Animal shelter
11. Machine storage
12. Barn, ca.1840

Eno River

↓

based on a map drawn
by Gabrielle McDermit

MONTROSE

INTRODUCTION

For most of my life I wondered what lay behind the fence covered with vines separating and hiding Montrose from St. Marys Road. When I was a child, my father drove our family in our old Studebaker to Hillsborough as a special treat. We always came into town along that road and I often saw men with picks, mattocks, and swing blades walking along the front edge of the property. They cleared away excess growth on the bank but didn't remove enough for us to see into the grounds.

My parents saw the garden the year the Grahams opened it for Hillsborough's spring tour. They didn't forget a detail. No matter where my husband, Craufurd, and I looked for a house, my father said, we should try to live at Montrose. He spoke of the rich, clay loam soil, the splendid old trees, and Mr. Graham's tomato frames. "With your love of gardening, you should move there." He repeated it again and again. "But it isn't for sale!" I protested.

Nature, especially plants, has always been the core of my life. My earliest and happiest childhood memories include the time when my parents discovered a patch of yellow lady slippers growing wild in Durham County. My parents had been so intent on finding the rare flowers, they weren't aware that we had wandered too close to a moonshine camp until we heard shots and realized that we were the targets. Even lady slippers aren't worth dying for. The first time we found atamasco lilies in a damp field near our house in Durham, a bull chased us all the way to the road. The sight of elegant white flowers tinged with pink growing in soggy soil was worth the heart-thumping run. When we reached the end of our five-hundred-(plus)-mile drives to visit my grandparents in middle Tennessee or south Georgia, we got out of the car and went straight into their gardens. The fact that we had driven for more than thirteen hours, had five or more flat tires, and hadn't eaten a bite for six hours paled in importance: we didn't wait a minute longer to see the newest plant or flower in bloom.

If you had land, you had a garden. You grew your food. You made the yard beautiful. And you talked about it. My earliest memory of my father has him behind our first house in Durham, North Carolina. He walked up to the house with a basket full of vegetables. I don't remember what they were, but I remember his pride. I must have been less than four years old. My favorite memory of my mother has her terribly excited about something in the garden behind our next house. I jumped from the swing and ran over to see her first blooming lady slipper. I was nearly six. We moved four times before my parents finally built the house they lived in for almost fifty years. For six years before we moved there, we spent every weekend at "the lot," where we pulled up honeysuckle and brambles, began the garden, sowed cover crops to improve the soil, and stuck cuttings of all the old plants they had admired. My father was not shy about asking for cuttings of trees or shrubs or divisions of old bulbs. My parents were teachers, my mother of fourth-grade children, and my father of English literature students at Duke University, but both revitalized themselves daily in their garden.

When I married Craufurd Goodwin in 1958, we moved to an apartment in Windsor, Ontario, where there was no land for a garden. I spent the year as a fine arts librarian but yearned for a plant. Few plants have given me greater pleasure than the garlic clove from the grocery store that I planted in a flower pot. From the moment the beige bulb sent up its first slender green leaf, I tended it and watched its daily transformation. We spent the following summer with Craufurd's mother, to whom I gave my plant and watched in agony as she ate it. Five years later we purchased our first house in Durham, and I had land of my own. I believed it would be my home for the rest of my life and I discovered quickly the beauty and mystery of gardening. I wanted to grow everything, so I studied seed catalogs, joined the

American Horticultural Society, and read all I could find on gardening. I couldn't absorb enough.

In those days I taught piano and harpsichord but never began to practice or to teach until I had walked through my garden. I put my favorite plants — hellebores, snowdrops, and primroses — near the music room window where I watched their progress and enjoyed their flowers when I was confined to the room. Many times I rushed back into the garden when the last student left to see whether the bud showing promise in early afternoon had opened while I was inside. Craufurd and I traveled during those years, often spending summers in England. When I couldn't sleep, I lay in total darkness mentally walking through my garden. I knew each bump in the paths and the location of every plant.

After three years, I ran out of space for the garden of my dreams and we began to look for a home with more land. We quickly narrowed our search to Orange County and waited for an appropriate property to come on the market. I was impatient. I saw my life flying by and I had not yet started my ultimate, my final garden. We spent nearly ten years looking for a property with more land. We examined development houses with five acres and mini-ranches with ten. Most of these had fancy bathrooms and at least one room (the "great" room) with a cathedral ceiling and they were built on gray or copper-red soil. We wanted better land for our garden and a comfortable house close to a town so we waited for a place near Hillsborough, a small, historic town only fourteen miles from Duke University, where Craufurd teaches. In winter we walked on the height of land behind Cameron Park School hoping to get a glimpse of Montrose but all we saw was a bit of gray slate roof. Occasionally we saw cars going up the winding drive, but we couldn't imagine what lay along and at the end of the road until April 1977, when Sandy (Alexander H.) Graham agreed to show us the property. His father, the last of the third generation of Grahams to live here, had died recently and he and his brother, John, needed to make a decision concerning their parents' place.

When Craufurd and I first drove through the gate at the entrance to Montrose that April, spring had barely begun. Young leaves were little more than green fluff on black branches. The house was spacious and bright even though the walls and ceilings in the living room and dining room were covered with green wallpaper embossed with ferns. The music room was lavender, and the kitchen walls covered with large images of bright white magnolias and brilliant red cardinals over a black background. We walked through the garden and saw potatoes emerging from the red-brown soil and fat spears of asparagus in a row south of an arbor overwhelmed by unpruned grapes. We walked through the law office, a six-room building directly behind the main house, and I fell in love. I could teach here and never disrupt the business of the house. When here, I felt as if I were in the midst of the garden. I told the Grahams I wanted to work on this land.

We left convinced that Montrose would be the perfect place for us, but the decision wasn't ours alone. We had to convince John and Sandy that we were the appropriate custodians of their family home. Craufurd has Graham ancestors going back to James Graham, the Marquis of Montrose, and we had his portrait in a little book written by Craufurd's grandmother. We noticed the same portrait on the living room wall at Montrose. This link made a difference, and within three months we came to an understanding with John and Sandy Graham. They agreed to sell us the property. It was the beginning of the greatest adventure of my life.

FIRST STEPS

Although we moved to Montrose in late summer 1977, I did very little with the garden until the following spring. I needed to know how the shadows lay, where the soil remained dry in times of normal moisture, and wet in times of drought. I needed to know what was already in place, and I needed to feel that I was more than a caretaker of the past. We didn't mind saying we lived at the old Graham place for the first ten years or so but now we say we live at Montrose.

We slowly made cosmetic changes to the interior of the house, repairs to the roof, and we painted the exterior of most of the buildings on the property. I continued to teach music and traveled from house to house in Durham three or four days a week. I longed to get into the garden. Several years later Craufurd and I painted two rooms in the law office behind the main house. This structure consisted of two early-nineteenth-century buildings joined together to form an office when Governor William Alexander Graham lived and practiced law on the property. He lived at Montrose with his family from 1842 until the early 1860s, when the house burned and he moved into Hillsborough, giving the property to his son, John. John built a second house that burned in the 1890s, but before he began to build the third house on that foundation, John enlarged the office, adding a wing so that his family could live there during the third construction of the house. Craufurd and I refinished the floors, installed a wood-burning stove, and I purchased a used Mason & Hamlin grand piano. After that, my students came to Hillsborough for lessons. Again I planted my favorites—snowdrops, early crocuses, and hellebores—outside the window of the room where I taught. I felt an enormous tug as if a large, powerful magnet were dragging me from the interior of the building into the garden. How could I revise my life? How could I

make some contribution to our life and spend most of my time outside? Teaching was the only profession for which I had any training.

I began to explore the garden and its potential and I wanted to grow as many different plants as I could. I searched catalogs and discovered that I could find only seeds for most of the plants I wanted to grow. I wanted all the little bulbs, the winter-flowering crocuses, and every species of cyclamen. I wanted every hardy geranium, salvia, and heuchera. Seeds germinated easily and I quickly built up a collection of cyclamen that, in a few years, produced their own seeds. A small mail-order nursery would surely provide the excuse I needed to escape into the garden every day. I could produce plants I had been unable to obtain and perhaps find people who, like me, were frustrated by the choices offered by big nurseries. They might buy my plants. I knew that, in the beginning, I would have to continue teaching but hoped that gradually the nursery would support itself and eventually provide enough income to pay for help in the nursery and garden. I began Montrose Nursery in 1984 with a few plants on my first mimeographed list. I packed plants in the morning, drove to UPS to ship them, then returned in time to heat the wood-burning stove and teach my students. It was the beginning of my release into the garden.

The nursery grew larger and larger and after two years I gave up teaching, sold the Mason & Hamlin piano, and found people to help with propagation and packing. Each year I wanted to make the list, now a little catalog, better and larger than the year before. I added more plants selected from the garden—plants not readily available from garden centers or other mail-order nurseries. Suddenly, I found myself, once again, in the law office, now converted to the shipping department. We shipped plants from Monday through Wednesday. At the end of the day on Wednesday, if we had filled all the orders and had no plants left over, we put a gold star on the calendar. This was for us an enormous achievement and we danced around the room at the end of each perfect shipping week. I sorted orders and plant labels for the next week's shipping on Thursday. Friday and Saturday we picked up plants to send out the following week. Sometimes we cleaned the plants and cyclamen pots on Saturday and Sunday. As soon as shipping season ended, I wrote the next catalog. I had two periods of about two weeks each for gardening—right after the catalogs were mailed the day before Christmas and shortly before the Fourth of July. Springs came and went when I didn't even walk through the garden. I felt the force of the magnet again. This time it was irresistible. There was only one solution. I closed the nursery ten years after opening it, put on my kneepads, and went back to the garden.

The days weren't what I thought they would be. Gardening is for me primarily a solitary occupation, one where I find peace and contentment with my hands in the dirt alone except for the sights and sounds of the creatures who share this land. I had by that time developed a garden larger than I could maintain alone. There were conflicts with the staff, problems finding people with a genuine interest in plants, the ability and willingness to work in all kinds of weather, a shared attitude toward this garden, and the humility to accept that ours is but a tiny part in its development. Prospective gardeners came and went. Some left voluntarily and others not but I knew that somewhere out there I would find compatible people who would respond to this garden as I do.

I do not want to live as a hermit. I needed to find a way to share the garden yet retain the necessary time to enjoy and tend it. I began with guided tours three days a week by appointment. By setting a regular schedule, I could group people together and still spend most of my time gardening. Around 1998 I began Garden Open Days when visitors can see the garden without a guided tour or fee and can purchase plants propagated from the garden. This works well. We have dates to work toward in spring and fall, times when most of the garden is weeded and mulched. These are periods when much of the garden looks its best, usually in late April or mid-May, and again at the end of September or early October.

I continue to search for balance, a way to return music and literature to my life. I listen to music but that isn't the same as the total involvement required to play an instrument. I prefer music for the harpsichord but rarely have more than the forty-five minutes necessary to tune my instrument. Every night I fall asleep with a book in hand but seldom have time to read during the day. This place is my life and its garden my obsession. I will run out of time before I have finished.

LATE JANUARY & FEBRUARY

In the winter of 2002, nine years after I closed Montrose Nursery, I began to keep a record of the year focusing primarily on the process of managing a four-season garden. I interspersed an account of what we found when we arrived at Montrose and how it has changed. The main characters are the plants that grow here, the people who tend them, and the animals, tame and wild, that live with us. Weather played an important role. I didn't know what plants, animals, or people would survive the year. I didn't know who would be here to help develop the garden and nurture the plants and animals at the end of the year—a brief cycle of twelve months with four overlapping seasons. We know when January ends and February begins but are uncertain when winter ends and spring begins.

I began 2002 with three part-time employees. Cathy Dykes first came to the garden in the spring of 2001. About five feet six inches with freckles, reddish-brown hair streaked with silver, she is soft-spoken, calm, and unpretentious. Small glasses cover her clear blue eyes when she works at the potting bench. She seems to float about the garden leaving each place she bends down to weed better than before. Bonnie Hutchinson came first to a Garden Morning, for a class in propagation and design, and joined the staff about a month later. She has a pleasant but reserved manner, an easy laugh, and looks dressed for an occasion in white shirts and rose-tinted glasses. Small barrettes control her curly brown hair. She has a good sense of color and design and is seldom dirty as she glides through the garden. Cheryl Traylor also came to that Garden Morning class. She helped as a volunteer during the spring and joined the staff the following August. She has bangs and medium brown hair pulled back into a ponytail. About five feet five inches with Italian features, she strides through the garden as if on a mission and works away at each task until it is finished. Her casual, comfortable manner and amusing sense of humor combine with a remarkably intuitive mind. She often gasps in wonder at the first sight of a plant in flower or a pot of newly germinated seeds. Ippy Patterson, friend and collaborator, lives about ten miles south of here. She sees and records nature with scientific accuracy and poetic lyricism. I met her first when she came for a tour of the garden about six years ago. She is tall, slender, and elegant with a clear, olive complexion and dark brown eyes. Her long, tapered fingers are always clean and her black hair with bits of white perfectly controlled. She looks like a model even in old clothes and moves silently through the garden, often coming to us across the gravel without our suspecting anyone is near. Wayne Hall, though not at Montrose during this year, is present through his work. A stocky, blond-haired man of about forty-five, he came in 1984 to help build the first greenhouse. During the next sixteen years he created most of the structures in the garden, laid out paths, made the house attractive and comfortable, and restored or converted all the buildings on the property. We admire his work and love his kind, competent manner, intelligence, and gentle spirit. He moved to Maine several years ago and we miss him still. Craufurd Goodwin, my husband of forty-three years, is chief lawn mower, kind but severe critic, and best friend. He works like a beaver to keep the beavers from destroying the pond with their dams. He helps keep the woods free of fallen trees and limbs. Impy, Stevie, and Cindy are seventeen-year-old cats; Beanie, age ten, and Tony, about seven, are their younger companions; and Roger is a frisky nine-month-old kitten.

I am a small person with short, gray hair, usually dressed in winter in faded jeans, frayed at the knees and cuffs, boots, and layers of old shirts, and in summer in faded shorts and shirts. A wide-brimmed straw hat without a crown protects my face from the sun. I generally pull a small aluminum cart loaded with a bucket filled with hand tools and a garden fork and spade as I walk briskly and look down to right or left at plants in growth or for those expected to grow. My hands are usually dirty, my knuckles somewhat distorted, and when I reach my destination, I work on hands and knees.

It is winter by the calendar, but spring by the air. The year moves forward, but the weather, like the tide, flows from one season to the next and back again. Winter plants, such as snowdrops and crocuses, show little damage after freezing nights; but cold nights may kill spring flowers of precocious arisaemas and other perennials in growth before their time. Warm, windy days that are so delightful to spend outside have an undercurrent of unease. I have learned to love this season and the blooms which appear long before they should. Even though many will be destroyed by cold, I am grateful to have seen them. This, the slow season, is my only time to linger over plants and look closely at each flower. Most winter days begin in the law office, where I write, read, and plan before going into the garden.

After I closed the nursery, we converted the law office into an office with a room for my horticultural library and meeting rooms for visitors, and installed part of our collection of Bloomsbury art. It became "A House of My Own," a private space where I read or write in silence and hold weekly staff meetings. Although the building has had many uses, it retains its original name, a reminder of those who were here before our time.

I gradually expanded the little garden surrounding the law office as I added more winter-flowering plants. Silvery white buds of *Edgeworthia papyrifera*, paper bush, at the base of the steps, begin to swell by midwinter. Few winters are reliable enough for the pendulous clusters of buds to open fully, but if I am lucky and they bloom, I may have seeds by summer and new plants a year later.

Corylopsis veitchiana (now *C. sinensis* var. *calvescens* f. *veitchiana*), on the west side of the law office, is laden with swollen, brown buds tinged with red or purple. Many of the outer cases have fallen away leaving pale chartreuse buds on twigs tinged with the dull blue-gray of lichen. If the weather holds, they will develop delicate tassels of lightly fragrant flowers, a gentle, refined alternative to the ubiquitous forsythia.

On cold days winter-flowering bulbs fill the greenhouses with fragrance so I often stop there before going into the garden. This year we celebrate the growth and bloom of *Tecophilaea cyanocrocus*, the Chilean blue crocus, first because of its beauty and rarity, and second because it is a new plant for us. A new flower is always the most special event of the day. In December a dark green spear, the color of pine trees in shade, emerged from the soil. This spear turned into a trio of leaves. In early January a flower emerged from the center of the cluster of leaves and opened slowly revealing six brilliant blue tepals. A tepal isn't a misspelled petal; it refers to a flower's petal-like segments that are botanically petals and sepals. The outer segments are most often sepals and the inner ones petals, so "tepals" includes both. The edge of each tepal of a Chilean crocus is the blue of a northern Italian lake. I have only one corm and must dry it off completely in summer to have a repeat performance next year.

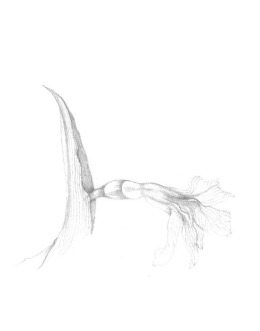

Tecophilaea cyanocrocus

In anticipation I feel the spears at the base of the leaf clusters of *Iris unguicularis* (*I. stylosa*) to find those fat enough to be flower buds. Although the straw-colored, vertical buds are difficult to see, it is worth the excitement of anticipation that precedes the purple, pink, or white flowers that gradually open each day. Behind the house the foliage on a seedling spreads out enough to reveal the flowers, but the leaves on most plants nearly hide them. A clump by the pump house, a small building that covers a well near the law office, produces medium purple flowers with darker, slender lines extending out from the center of the standards. I pass a paintbrush gently over the pollen and then stroke the stigma to produce seeds that ripen at ground level in late spring.

Iris unguicularis flower

Round, bright yellow buds of winter aconites, *Eran-this hyemalis*, show up against the brown mulch opposite the Dianthus Walk that leads to the front door of the house. Curled stems seem to pull the flowering stalks up from below ground. Tripartite leaves with feathered tips are chartreuse green below and medium green above. Soon the flowers will open wide in sun but close again into round buds at night.

Hamamelis x *intermedia* 'James Wells' looks a bit scruffy now with its old beige leaves hiding the swollen flower buds, so with sharp clippers I cut away the papery brown leaves. They seem to be holding on for dear life and cannot be torn away without damaging the flowers. With magnification I see a furry calyx with golden hairs protecting the flower that now shows its true color — bright yellow. Hints of the brilliant red underside of the calyx make the bud glow from within. A day later the flowers expand into wisps of yellow. The red of the calyx is more visible, and the plant becomes a twiggy shrub decorated with narrow, wrinkled ribbons. Farther along at the south end of the Circle Garden, the pale yellow flowers of *H.* x *i.* 'Primavera' have less visible red calyxes making them a haze of primrose yellow while *H.* x *i.* 'Jelena' has butterscotch flowers with dark crimson bases. These witch hazels obligingly drop all their leaves so I just breathe in their subtle fragrance and admire their flowers.

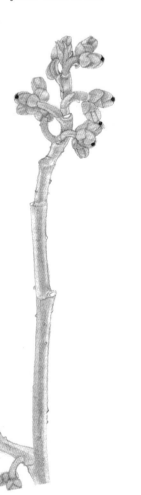

Hamamelis x *intermedia* 'James Wells' in bud

Hamamelis x *intermedia* 'Jelena'

Cornus sanguinea 'Winter Beauty', *Chamaecyparis obtusa* 'Limerick', and *Nandina domestica*

Nandinaland, a border at the curve of the driveway as it leads to the parking lot, is a feature at this season. Bronze-foliaged, shrubby nandinas (*Nandina domestica*) topped with drooping clusters of deep red berries provide the background of the bed behind Paul Jones's seedling, *Chamaecyparis obtusa* 'Limerick' with its bright, chartreuse yellow needles. Paul, a friend and curator of the William Culberson Asiatic Arboretum at Duke University, had for several years a small and distinguished nursery, "Fascinations," specializing in unusual woody plants. Many of the rarest conifers at Montrose came from Paul. Even on cloudy days 'Limerick' looks as if a spotlight is shining directly on it. The coral stems of *Cornus sanguinea* 'Winter Beauty' show up against it and *Hypericum kouytchense*, in the midst of the dogwoods, retains leaves which are the same soft coral of the multi-stemmed dogwood. Near the edge of this planting, *Yucca flaccida* 'Wilder's Wonderful' provides a spiky rosette with medium yellow and green striped leaves bearing streaks of coral at the tips.

When we came to Montrose, ivy lined the brick walk leading to the front door of the house, an ivy supposedly so rare and tender that we found wooden covers specifically constructed to protect it in winter. I never used them and discovered that the ivy was neither rare nor tender; in fact it survived temperatures around minus nine degrees Fahrenheit during our most severe winter. It didn't grow well in that location, perhaps because it received too much sun. We removed these plants from their stony soil and replaced them with our favorite heat-tolerant dianthus cultivars, including 'Inchmery', 'Essex Witch', 'Fair Folly', 'Lady Gran-ville', 'Painted Beauty', 'Queen of Sheba', and 'Ursula Le Grove'. We added creeping phloxes and other low-growing perennials and mulched the bed with gravel. After more than ten years, the dianthus became a disheveled, sprawling mass of thread-like stems with flimsy foliage. We restored the Dianthus Walk this year. Craufurd agreed to let me close the roadway for a week, and four tons of small stones (gravel screenings) were deposited just beyond the brick path. We weeded slowly and carefully, trying to re-move every tiny scrap of unwanted veronica, oxalis, and chickweed from the beds. Then we hauled the stones in buckets, shovels, and wheelbarrows and scattered them over the wispy stems of dianthus and phlox, finally carrying the remaining gravel to the Scree Garden near the greenhouse. New roots formed in the stony mulch and tufts of bright green or silvery blue leaves quickly appeared above the new gray base.

Many woody plants transplant most successfully in February because they have time to settle in before they put on new growth. We moved a large *Abelia* 'Edward Goucher' from the edge of the big greenhouse to the burgundy and silver section of the sunny gardens. A variegated Chinese holly, *Ilex cornuta* 'O. Spring', went from beneath the buddlejas in the shrub border in the main sunny gardens to the top of the wall south of the Blue and Yellow Garden. We took turns, one holding the shrub in place and the other stepping away, to determine the correct location of each plant. *Yuccas filamentosa* 'Variegata', Adam's needles, were transplanted to the corners of several sunny gardens and *Mahonia repens*, hidden behind the boxwoods, where I first put it almost twenty-five years earlier, was moved to the base of the purple-leaf peaches.

February is the month for hellebores that grow along the Mother-in-Law Walk, at the top of the first woodland terrace. This path, filled with memories of those no longer alive, is a main feature of the winter garden with none of the unpleasant overtones accompanying many mother-in-law stories. I

Narcissus

began to plant the area on either side of the path in 1986 with a few bulbs we found on the kitchen counter after Craufurd's mother died. She had purchased them the fall of her final illness. My mother died in 1992 and before I sold her house, I brought trilliums, bloodroot, selaginella, and little wood hyacinths (now *Hyacinthoides hispanica*) from her woods. In 1996 J. C. Raulston, director of the North Carolina State Arboretum, gave me a handsome selection of the White Magic strain of *Helleborus niger*, which I planted along the walk, not realizing that he, too, would die tragically in an automobile accident within the month. I added more Christmas roses along the edges of the path and this winter planted a mass of them on the hillside above. I can imagine how this section will look in years to come—a slope covered in mid-winter with white-flowering plants, all facing south and west. Although this special part of the woods garden is filled with memories of friends and past times, only occasionally do I feel sad when I work here. In early April when the wildflowers bloom, I feel the presence of my mother. I wish for another visit with her the way she was before her final illness. I long to lead her down this path where I know she would stop to examine every living thing—weeds included.

Exquisite *Helleborus niger* comes in a variety of flower shapes with subtle differences in color. Some sepals (petals) have pink backs, some turn pink as they age, and others have touches of green. Some flowers have large, green nectaries at the base of the petals and pink stigmas that add a blush to the center of the flower. The center, composed of many stamens, tightly packed at first, expands as the pollen ripens into dusty yellow. The large flowers on J. C.'s *H. niger* turn rose-pink shading to green at the center with pink-tipped carpels (seed capsules).

Helleborus purpurascens grows on the steep bank away from the main planting of hybrids where I hope they are far enough from other species to breed true. I want a large drift of them, each with slate-blue flowers, and each a little different from its neighbor.

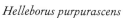

Helleborus purpurascens

Helleborus x *hybridus*, picotee strain

The picotee strain of hellebore hybrids selected years ago for their beautiful shading and dark nectaries grow in isolation near the pond at the foot of the hill. Overlapping sepals form a shallow cup shaded from dark purple to chartreuse cream surrounding a central crown of pale yellow stamens above a ring of dark red-violet nectaries. The exterior looks as if it were painted with dark red-violet finger paints.

Five species of hellebores with green or nearly green flowers grow in the shady gardens. Except for size *H. cyclophyllus* and *H. odorus* are barely distinguishable from each other. Both have chartreuse flowers but the former seems a giant beside the latter. *H. viridis*, another green-flowered species, is self-cleaning with old leaves that shrivel away in early winter and bloom stalks that appear shortly thereafter. More green-flowered hellebores grow beneath and around *Mahonia* x *wagneri* 'King's Ransom' near the old wood splitter across from the potting room. One group of *H. torquatus* has bright green stalks and small green flowers and bracts, but a superior form nearby produces sepals with backs almost as dark as the mahonia leaves and green interiors with burgundy edges. *H. mul-*

tifidus subsp. *hercegovinus*, growing closer to the wood splitter, has pendulous, green flowers without a hint of purple and finely dissected leaves. The flowers, surrounded by finely divided green bracts, open fully before the leaves appear. A final green-flowered hellebore, diminutive *H. dumetorum*, along the Mother-in-Law Walk, has stalks bearing upturned flowers nestled in leafy bracts only three or four inches above the soil. All its flowers are similar—clear, medium green shading to near-white at the very edge of each sepal and with a small circle of near-white stamens in the center of each bloom. The many-segmented leaves are blue-green, or green tinged with purple. This hellebore disappears by mid-summer and reappears in mid-winter. I have five blooming-sized plants, one of which was so small a *Cyclamen coum* hid it from view until now. It seems extraordinary to think a cyclamen could hide a hellebore.

Below the large rocks near the northern edge of the woods grow a large group of dark-flowered hellebore hybrids, the descendants of a superb form given to me by William Lanier Hunt, a gardener and writer in Chapel Hill. I crossed his plant with a seedling strain received erroneously as *H. atrorubens*. Their flowers in shades of red-violet, magenta-purple, and rose-purple remind me of visits to Bill's hillside clothed with hellebores, cyclamen, and rare bulbs of all sorts. Bill always put me to shame when I visited his garden, for he climbed his steep hill quickly without panting, while I, about thirty years younger, clambered slowly up to the top gasping for breath. He usually wore a bow tie and had a flower in his lapel, and he seldom saw a plant he didn't know. I invited Bill to wander around the garden whenever he wanted and he came often. I knew he was here when I saw his old brown car parked in the driveway.

The pink flowers of *H. thibetanus*, a recently discovered species, nestle in the top of a cluster of medium silvery-green, leafy bracts lined with delicate maroon veins. An early bloomer, it grows below the Mother-in-Law Walk where I can cross it with *H. niger*.

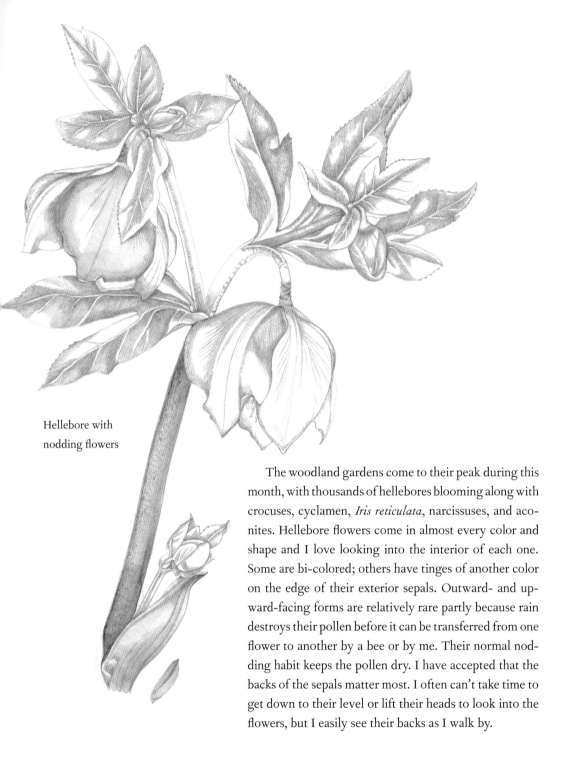

Hellebore with
nodding flowers

The woodland gardens come to their peak during this month, with thousands of hellebores blooming along with crocuses, cyclamen, *Iris reticulata*, narcissuses, and aconites. Hellebore flowers come in almost every color and shape and I love looking into the interior of each one. Some are bi-colored; others have tinges of another color on the edge of their exterior sepals. Outward- and upward-facing forms are relatively rare partly because rain destroys their pollen before it can be transferred from one flower to another by a bee or by me. Their normal nodding habit keeps the pollen dry. I have accepted that the backs of the sepals matter most. I often can't take time to get down to their level or lift their heads to look into the flowers, but I easily see their backs as I walk by.

I cut away the hellebore's old tattered leaves for three reasons. First, so they don't hide the flowers; and second, to prevent the spread of fungal diseases seen or unseen. Perhaps the third reason is best. When I crawl about the woodland gardens, I see emerging buds and each opened flower above its carpet of dried leaves and can select plants to hand pollinate. Open-pollinated flowers often produce inferior plants. Armed with a basket containing scissors, string, a fine paintbrush, clippers, labels, and a pencil, I clip off a flower with ripe, dusty pollen, pull back the sepals, and brush its anthers across the stigma of a flower with tightly clustered anthers. I tie a string on the pedicel (stem) of the pollinated flower and place a label with information about the cross at the base of the plant. I want dark flowers, early bloomers, late bloomers, pure pinks, yellows, whites, apricots, flowers that face outward, nectaries that are dark. I will have them more quickly if I make the crosses.

Hellebore bud

Tony and Roger often accompany me when I go down the road to the pond to pollinate hellebores. Tony, a portly male tabby cat, agreed to live with us about four years ago. I noticed him slinking about the garden for several years before attempting to tame him. He is a handsome cat with a peaceful disposition. Tufts of fur emerge from the top of his large, pointed ears and his coat, now a little tight, almost looks like it's made of polyester. We named him for our good friend Tony Bradshaw, in England — the only person we know who gets along with everyone. Our Tony gets along with all the old female cats, as well as Beanie, our other large male. He accepts Roger as an equal playmate.

Ippy draws each plant or flower at eye level, so we tried a new experiment so she could have perfect hellebores in vases in a warm room rather than having to lie before them on the cold ground. She wanted to illustrate the *H.* x *sternii* hybrids that grow beneath the pines. This hybrid, *H. lividus* crossed with *H. argutifolius*, grows best where the needles above give it some protection. We cut the flowers and plunged their stems immediately into a bucket of warm water and then returned to the house where we cut them again under running water, put them into fresh warm water, and added a little isopropyl alcohol. It worked. They did not dangle in a limp mass as all the others picked in past years did. They looked as fresh at the end of the day as they had when we first saw them in the garden.

Helleborus x *sternii*

Crocuses join hellebores in the winter garden. Only the ghostly white buds and perianth tubes of the Tommies, *Crocus tommasinianus*, show up in the dim morning and evening light. A hint of the color of their interiors shows at the tip of each bud before the sun causes it to open completely. Before the month ends we have masses of white, dark purple, and red-violet forms in flower. *C. vernus* and its hybrids bloom throughout the woodland gardens and *C. sieberi*, with flowers in shades of purple or pure white, grows along the driveway. The first year here we found a clump of golden crocuses (probably *Crocus flavus*) like massed cups of gold near the large juniper at the edge of the field.

Crocus vernus

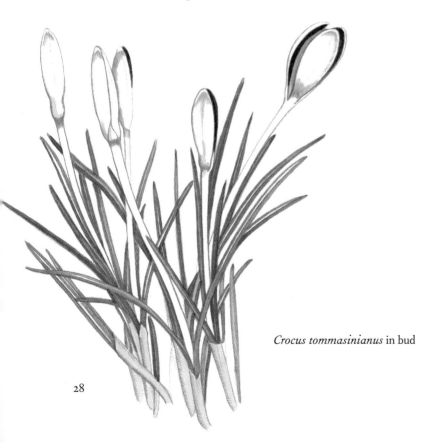

Crocus tommasinianus in bud

Snowdrops (*Galanthus sp.*) open quickly in February. Warm days bring most forms of *G. elwesii* into flower and clumps of *G. nivalis* above the leaf litter. Leaves like little spears tightly pressed together protect the flower within. Some leaves unfold one from within another while others rise flat, one against the other. A papery spathe that covers and protects the bud lengthens until the opened flower dangles beneath it. Although I grow some double-flowering forms, I prefer the single ones. I search for the first sight of each clump of snowdrops and marvel at the subtle variations of each form. Some of the outer petals (tepals) have spots of green and the inner cups may be all green, have x-shaped patterns of green, or small green bands at their tips.

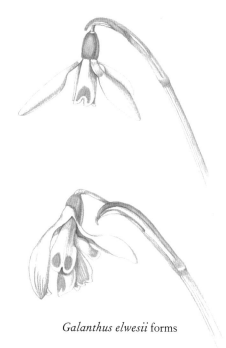

Galanthus elwesii forms

This February I hope to plant a Snowdrop Walk. Earlier in the month I dug out maple seedlings south of a flat path about four feet wide at the edge of the woods. The path curves, following the ridge of land shaded by massive poplars, maples, and dogwoods, and is so long I can't see from one end to the other. I wondered just how long a walk I had made and began several times at one end or the other counting my steps. I had to do this again and again for invariably I found my attention wandering as I noticed hellebores in bud and newly emerged bulbs in neighboring beds. I think the new Snowdrop Walk is nearly two hundred and fifty feet long. As *Galanthus nivalis* appeared along the driveway, I dug and replanted them at six- to

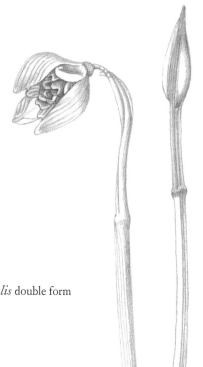

Galanthus nivalis double form

eight-inch intervals in a six-foot-wide bed south of the new path. Often the clumps I dug had multiplied so much that some bulbs grew on top of others. It took nearly a month to divide and plant the snowdrops, after which I edged the bed with my tightest, slowest-growing form of mondo grass, *Ophiopogon japonicus*, and planted the east end with small sprigs of sweet box, *Sarcococca hookeriana* var. *humilis*, closely spaced, so that they will eventually form a boundary to this garden. The birds complained the entire time I worked, perhaps because I was often accompanied by a cat. A Carolina wren, several tomtits, and chickadees all seemed perturbed by my presence. By the end of February the walk looked thinly carpeted — perhaps with a moth-eaten carpet — but I imagine future springs with quivering masses of green and white nodding flowers no more than six or eight inches above ground. I don't mind waiting fifty-one weeks for one week of glory. The anticipation will enhance the moment.

As I plan the expansion of the woodland gardens, I think of those who worked this soil before me. The house and buildings are at about six hundred and fifty feet above sea level and the southern boundary of the property is the meandering bank of the Eno River at the bottom of the hill. According to the 1977 Soil Survey of Orange County, Hillsborough is outside the Great Triassic Basin, and the upland soil, where our gardens are, consists of a somewhat acidic Georgeville silt loam, formed from volcanic slates, above a clay subsoil. During the 1930s the Grahams terraced most of the woodland for erosion control, in order to grow crops in the floodplain. It would have been painful for me to see large trees cut and the earth moved about. I would have hated to lose the natural vegetation and topsoil, but there are compensations. The south-facing hillside is contoured with gentle slopes flattening out to level ground, perfect for paths. Below the paths short, steep banks and ridges lead to the next slope. This pattern is repeated all the way down to the floodplain, now carpeted with spring beauties (*Claytonia virginica*) and dog-toothed violets (*Erythronium umbilicatum*). Seventy-year-old maples, beeches, oaks, sweet gums, hickories, and walnuts that tower over dogwoods and redbuds provide summer shade.

Respecting the past, I see no need to reshape it or to add artificial waterfalls. The terracing done many years ago provides me with a hillside that isn't eroding away. The earlier manipulation of the terrain was done carefully based on the topography of the land, even though I doubt the Grahams foresaw the development in this area that now produces almost yearly floods. During our time here, the water has never risen to the top of the lowest terrace. The place and those who preceded us dictate the shape, if not the actual contents, of this garden.

The woodland with its informal, naturalized plantings is the soul of my garden. I have more plans for the woods south and west of the new Snowdrop Walk. Periwinkle and seedling maples and beeches grow beneath majestic old trees not touched by the reconfiguration of the land. First we must clear away the undergrowth that obscures the massive tree trunks and then I hope to underplant the large poplars, maples, and oaks with drought-resistant, shade-loving, winter-flowering bulbs including snowdrops, aconites, and crocuses; shrubs, including mahonias, daphnes, and rhododendrons; and perennials, including hellebores, primulas, and epimediums. When we clear this area, we will have a woods walk leading to the edge of our highest ridge where we look out over the floodplain. The planting is less important than the clearing. Even if we add no plants, we will extend the view and see the natural beauty of the forest. Sometimes fewer plants provide the greatest beauty and serenity.

Adonis amurensis

Adonis amurensis remains closed in early morning, although the stalk has lengthened to about three inches. Purple sepals that covered the buds when they first pushed through the rocky soil have fallen away and the flowers open in sun above leaves that look like finely dissected bronze collars. The bright yellow flowers look a little like polished, refined dandelions.

Daffodils planted many years ago appear in February near the field west of the boxwoods where they must have been placed in a furrow made with a plough, for the bulbs grow in long, straight rows. Three generations of Grahams preceded us and left old bulbs, mature trees and shrubs, a long serpentine border of boxwoods, *Buxus sempervirens* 'Suffruticosa', and a beautifully laid out vegetable garden. When we arrived we found the remnants of an old rock garden, a long, dry stone wall, and the terraced woodland. Our first year was the grandest treasure hunt. We didn't know what we would find that hot day in July when we agreed to buy Montrose from John and Sandy Graham.

In the Rock Garden small daffodils with clear yellow trumpets and paler primrose-yellow petals look awkward. The flower seems too large for its four-inch stalk. Proportion matters most in miniature plants. The elegant swan's neck narcissus, *N. moschatus*, now open at the edge of the woods, grew in this garden before we arrived. I was thrilled to discover it for until then it was only a name in a book. Lightly drooping flowers open from chartreuse yellow buds surrounded by translucent beige spathes. At first opening the lightly fluted cup is clear yellow and the corolla pale creamy yellow with faint streaks of chartreuse on the back of each petal. The flowers grow paler as they mature until finally they are nearly white with touches of yellow. Silvery green leaves distinguish them from their bright yellow relatives even before they bloom. After dividing the clumps for many years, now at last we have a few drifts.

Narcissus moschatus

34

On the north side of the path leading to the big greenhouse a clump of *Narcissus fernandesii* blooms with pairs of intensely fragrant, bright yellow flowers on stems nearly six inches high. Short cups curve slightly inward and pointed petals have whitish tips. The blooming stems rise above bright green leaves, almost as narrow as an onion's. Another clump in the middle of a ferocious *Opuntia humifusa* keeps me at a distance. That cactus can protect anything!

Narcissus fernandesii

Winter-flowering cyclamen add brilliance to the winter garden. *Cyclamen alpinum*, formerly *C. trochopteranthum*, at the base of the large white oak in the Rock Garden, has elegant, propeller-like flowers that look too delicate to be as hardy as they are. Vivid magenta, pale pink, or white flowers brighten the dried oak leaves and bits of bark that cover the ground. *Cyclamen coum* blooms in all of the woods gardens, but is most appreciated beneath the metasequoias east of the house. At first I grew only silver leaf forms there, but many plants of the later generations have green patterns on their leaves. Special strains of *C. coum* grown from Roger Poulet's seeds grow along the road to the pond. Intense magenta flowers and well-marked leaves distinguish his plants from all others. They remind me of the nursery days and my excitement at discovering what forms I had grown from seed.

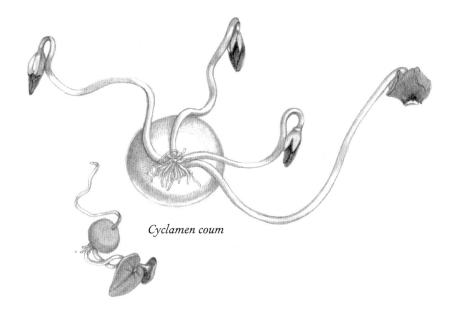

Cyclamen coum

Mr. Poulet, a keen English plantsman, wrote excellent letters and shared seeds of some of his best plants. We were only pen pals, but I hope to visit his garden someday and I think of him when I see his cyclamen. The seedlings from the Cyclamen Society's expedition to Turkey also grow in isolation. These flowers are either deepest magenta or pure white without any marking at the mouth of the flower. The strains from Russian seeds, in another section of the garden, have heart-shaped leaves and are usually the first to bloom, often by Thanksgiving.

Cyclamen was a genus in trouble at the time I started my nursery. Most plants available from nurseries were wild-collected and the mortality rate was high. The tubers collected in Turkey were often indistinguishable from each other and many tender and rare species were sent out with incorrect names. Largely through the efforts of the Cyclamen Society the public has learned of their precarious position in their native habitats, and international regulations have slowed the export of illegally collected plants. My original plants were grown from seeds from that society, the Royal Horticultural Society, or from friends, and all of my plants since then have come from my own seeds. I found them easy to grow and discovered a ready market of eager gardeners hoping for success with these charming flowers.

This warm February lures deciduous magnolias into bloom. *Magnolia* x *loebneri* 'Merrill' is almost at its peak at the edge of the field along the driveway leading to our house. I planted our tree, now about twenty feet tall, shortly after moving here. Pink buds with a raspberry stripe on the exterior of the tepals open to fragrant, near-white flowers. I know a freeze will destroy these opened flowers but more buds remain protected by their gray, furry calyxes, soft as a kitten and the color of Roger, our youngest cat. Roger often works with me in the garden. He has a coat of the finest silk with a few delicate stripes and spots and little beige ears. He is a good companion and sits near where I work sometimes helping with the digging.

Magnolia x *loebneri*

Occasionally we play tag, or hide-and-seek, or we dance. He turns sideways, stiff-legged, puffs up the hair on his back and tail, and prances. I'm not so graceful, but I also turn sideways and prance. We prefer to do this out of sight of others. Roger keeps an eye on me and cries if I get out of sight, which seldom happens.

Cats are perfect garden companions. They are neither noisy nor talkative, and lie nearby patiently waiting for the next little trip to the compost or brush piles and the final trip into the house for dinner. Sometimes my work is too boring for them or my location too hot or cold, but their natural curiosity and gentle disposition add tranquility to my tasks and I feel honored when they stay with me. Often they alert me to the presence of others, whether people, other cats, snakes, insects, or birds. They usually see them first.

Fragrant flowering shrubs perfume the garden. Wintersweet, *Chimonanthus praecox* var. *luteus*, at the back of Nandinaland, fills the cedar walk with its luscious smell. The musky, honey smell of sweet box, *Sarcococca hookeriana* var. *humilis*, permeates the woods and the Circle Garden that surrounds the Rock Garden. Small off-white flowers are barely noticeable until I kneel to them. The winter honeysuckle, *Lonicera fragrantissima*, began to bloom in December and continues to produce popcorn-like flowers that remind me of my parents' garden. The fragrance of the large rosemary in bloom near the gate leading to the greenhouse suggests savory stews. *Prunus mumes*, Japanese apricots, spice the air wherever they grow — in the woods and near the buildings. The delicious fragrance of *Daphne odora* makes crawling about in the woods to cut away hellebore leaves a heady experience. *Cyclamen coum*, *Viola odorata*, *Galanthus elwesii*, *Iris unguicularis*, many small narcissus, and most crocuses with more delicate scents force me down to their level. I can't describe most of them, but think snowdrops smell like spring rain. Even *Mahonia japonica*, grape holly, though fragrant, lures me closer to smell it.

Clumps of a hardy, white-flowering *Verbena canadensis* provide the greatest surprise as they bloom in winter along the walk into the center of the Circle Garden. All the seedlings of this verbena have similar large clusters of pure white flowers, bright green leaves, and relatively upright growth. Large clumps of pale yellow-flowered winter aconites, *Eranthis hyemalis*, bloom nearby and, although they don't show up as well as the brilliant yellow ones, I prefer their gentle color. Perhaps someday I will find white ones.

In late winter a group of oriental arborvitaes, *Platycladus orientalis* 'Juniperoides', look like a fairy forest with bronze-green needles and silvery-blue tips. Chartreuse stems of the shrubby American dogwoods, *Cornus sericea* 'Flaviramea', next to them, show up against their dark conical shapes. Black-leaved clumps of the lesser celandine, *Ranunculus ficaria* 'Brazen Hussy', have come into growth and a black flower has opened on a viola nearby. In another month the chartreuse leaves of creeping jenny will turn from winter brown to spring chartreuse.

January jasmine, *Jasminum nudiflorum*, justifies its name with clear yellow flowers along leafless branches. I can coax nearly bare branches into bloom inside if I pick them as soon as I see a hint of red in the flower bud, but there has been no need for that this year. They have bloomed constantly. Graceful wands of branches curve over each other, root where they touch the ground, and must be removed before they form new plants and smother their neighbors.

Above the jasmine, *Clematis cirrhosa* clings to the bark of an old red cedar, *Juniperus virginiana*. This fragrant, winter-flowering clematis began to bloom in November and endures almost any weather. It's easy to look up into the speckled interior of translucent, pale yellow, bell-like flowers as they dangle from slender stems. Young, round seed clusters of white feathery tails look like tiny puffs of cotton set among the shiny, dark green leaves tinged with bronze.

Clematis cirrhosa

A group of short nandinas at the corner of the bank near the garage has small, red berries that brighten their slender leaves, now dark green, bronze, and red. Every year I grow a few seeds from these plants and the resulting plants are all small with needle-like foliage, each different from the others.

The giant fennel, *Ferula communis*, has new feathery leaves on foot-high stalks and *Iris reticulata* has opened its first clear blue flower. It doesn't really matter that I don't know the cultivar names of the ones I grow. They are just as lovely without names. Additional forms with flowers in shades of purple, blue, and red-violet will bloom before March.

Even on cold days bluebirds sing their gentle, warbling song without seeming to take breath. A tomtit sits on the edgeworthia outside the law office and I hear the repetitive, but pleasant, song from a towhee in the *Prunus mume* (Japanese apricot) near the big greenhouse. We hear the owls conversing around four in the afternoon. They sing some duets but in general, a dialogue of solos. Their timing is perfect; one ends as the other begins. I recognize one as the young owl we first heard three or four years ago. He seems to be tone deaf and has trouble with the endings of his sentences. Flickers go into the loft of the barn late every evening. The board that juts out on the west side supported a pulley to help lift hay into the second floor of the barn but is little more than a stub now, just right for a bird to land on before slipping through the little hole. Woodpeckers peck away at the trees in the woods, calling for mates.

Cedar waxwings fill the branches of the large hackberry tree, *Celtis occidentalis*, beside the house and squeal with delight as they devour the berries. This tree is sometimes called a sugarberry tree so, knowing the fruit isn't poisonous, I tasted a berry. True, it isn't poison but neither is it worth eating. Cardinals sing their spring, warbling songs and vireos hop about low in the January jasmine. I saw Roger pounce on something and hoped in vain it was a rodent, but when I discovered the truth, I pounced on the cat and he dropped a white-eyed vireo. Craufurd put Roger in the house and I ran to the potting room for the bird box—a large shoebox lined with soft tissues and pierced for air holes. I picked up the warm, motionless bird, astonished by how light and fragile he seemed. We put him into the box, put the lid on, and placed the box on my counter in the potting room. Several hours later I took the box to the platform of the woodsplitter, opened the lid away from me, and watched with delight as he flew to the highest branch of the deciduous holly nearby.

The peeling bark of the chestnut rose, *Rosa roxburghii* f. *normalis*, hangs in shreds from horizontal branches but peels away from the main trunk, revealing fresh new bark beneath. This massive plant, now grown into a small tree, is literally a thorn in the side of the mower. Fierce protective thorns on these old Chinese roses mean we must cut them back for Craufurd's protection when he mows and for harmony in the home. We will remove the lower, spreading branches.

Impy, our smallest old cat, has made a new bed in the base of a large, empty iron cooking pot. She curls up there out of the wind and out of sight of predators. We spent many fretful moments before finding her there, but now we know where to look Impy is deaf, so calling her does no good.

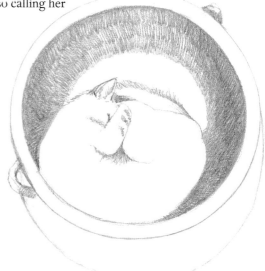

Deer often come to the garden for food in mid-winter. They graze at the side of the little greenhouse attached to the main house. They prefer my largest arborescent ivy, *Hedera helix* f. *poetarum* 'Poetica Arborea', and strip the plant of leaves and berries leaving only crooked sticks to leaf out again in spring.

I work outside until after six now that the days are longer. When I go in, I am accompanied by the cats, who race for the house as I go toward it. Roger usually gets there first. Beanie and Tony are next, and the old females last. Tony grooms the males. Beanie goes up to him and gives a little head bump as greeting, then bows his head just below Tony's chin. Tony washes him thoroughly. Now Roger has learned how to do it and stands with bowed head until he, also, is washed.

Epimediums begin to bloom in February. Barrenwort is their inappropriate common name; they aren't barren at all. Seedlings, many with fine flowers, appear throughout the shady gardens. I will remove the old foliage of all epimediums before the new flower stalks are so high that I cut them by mistake. I think I could do this blindfolded. The stalks with old leaves are stiff and the new ones are hairy and soft. I wait until the last possible moment for this task, for they delineate the woodland paths and when the old leaves are gone, visitors won't know where to step. Even I won't know where to step. *E. grandiflorum* 'Queen Esta' is among the first to open its pinkish purple flowers. These are the days when I go about the garden in circles. I see plants as they emerge from dormancy, and they remind me of others that should be visible but haven't yet been seen. So off I go in search of them.

In the Old Garden at the edge of the woods below the Aster Border, *Colchicum hungaricum* f. *albiflorum* bears its small white flowers with charcoal anthers just above the ground. The first flower appeared at Christmas and now, two months later, I have just seen its last flower for this season. My one and only *Helleborus vesicarius* grows near the *Maclura pomifera*, osage orange, at the back of the bed. This rare, choice species suffered greatly in my garden, so about five years ago I moved the remnant of my original plant to this new location, where the soil is hot and dry in summer when it is dormant. Three clusters of blooms this year give hope of seeds.

Craufurd cut three large willows to the ground. This was a difficult decision, for our plants had begun to show the first signs of spring growth. The largest, *Salix alba* var. *sericea*, overwhelmed the shrub border in the sunny gardens; it was too tall and too wide. If we hadn't done this the year before, I would have found it even more difficult, but when trees outgrow their places we have no other choice. Last summer after drastic pruning in February, we had shrubs six feet high by September and I expect the same to happen this year.

We cleared off the Aster Border, the southwest corner of the sunny gardens. We cut away the old aster stalks and thinned the plants, removing those impinging on their more delicate neighbors. Blackened and browned grasses and shrubs remain, but the fresh, green rosettes of the asters in and around their bases are ready to grow. Most of last year's growth on half-hardy salvias was left in the hope that they survive the winter but the ghostly silver stalks of Russian sage, *Perovskia atriplicifolia*, was left because they are attractive. The transformation of a little bit of this garden invigorated us and we began mulching with shredded leaves delivered by our local sanitation department.

The coldest part of each morning is spent potting on seedlings of spring annuals. We save seeds of our best plants every year and have a fine collection of special color forms. I wish I could sow them in place but the thick mulch, spread to keep moisture in and weeds out, prevents germination of desirable seeds as well. Poppies, calendulas, purple-leaved mustard, and bachelor buttons will go into the cold frame to harden off and into the garden as soon as the weather warms. There they will bloom quickly after transplanting and provide an almost instant show.

I planted a group of small *Dianthus erinaceus*, grown from seeds collected shortly before my original plant expired last summer. I put them into the Scree Garden, a gravelly bed between the parking lot and big greenhouse, where, in my mind's eye, I see a drift of small pink flowers above blue-gray tufts in the near future. I dug snowdrops and alliums displaced by our division of a large, gracefully arching clump of sapphire-blue-berried ophiopogon, *Ophiopogon ohwii*, planted years ago. Earlier this winter we took two garden forks back to back, divided clumps of this ophiopogon into several pieces, and planted them where the dark green mounds will intensify the purple-black foliage of *Mahonia* x *wagneri* 'King's Ransom' growing nearby.

Shortly before he left, Wayne Hall constructed a pair of "canopy beds," low trellises, nine feet by six feet with corner posts only three feet high, and topped them with arching pieces of juniper that cross each other to form an x. They support roses intertwined with clematis and help to separate the May Garden from the Shrub Border in the sunny gardens. For several years I tried to manage pink-flowering multiflora roses on the easternmost one, cutting away the longest canes and trying to train others to the juniper branches. No matter how drastically I pruned them, the roses threw new branches into the air, into the shrubs nearby, and into the rest of the beds. They insisted on remaining unruly so we decided to dig them out.

We approached our task cautiously, cutting away small pieces until we could reach the larger branches with loppers. Several hours later the plants were skeletons of their former selves and with a mattock and deep shovel we dug them out. Our strength came from chocolate bars we consumed in honor of Valentine's Day. Our pleasure came from working together and succeeding with what originally seemed an enormous, perhaps impossible, task.

Few visitors tour our garden in winter although there is much to see and time to appreciate it. Last fall, just after I accepted an appointment for a group to come in mid-February, I began to worry about the weather. Would we have the record snow of the new millennium? Would an unprecedented cold snap destroy all the flowers that can withstand normal temperatures but not temperatures below five degrees? The day was perfect, cold and sunny. A small cluster of people, wearing sensible shoes, walked briskly up the drive and exclaimed over the aconites, crocuses, and hellebores blooming in the Rock Garden. "You have flowers!" one man declared. I knew by their shoes, the way they walked, and the things they noticed that this would be a stimulating and appreciative group. We visited the Circle Garden with its architectural plants: *Sabal minor* (hardy palm), *Yucca flaccida*, *Euphorbia* x *martini*, and *Poncirus trifoliata* 'Flying Dragon' (trifoliate orange). The honeyed scent of sweet box and daphne filled the air. We went to the woods in small groups because of hazards such as stumps, roots, or holes in the paths. Bonnie led one group and Cathy and I the other. No one stepped on the many desirable self-sown plants that grow in the paths. This group, the perfect beginning to our tour season, consisted of real gardeners. Some grow mostly vegetables, others grow flowers, and many want to grow everything desirable that this climate and their space allow. We were with friends. The light changed before the month ended. In early morning when I walked up the hill after picking up the paper, I no longer saw dim variations of gray in the early morning sky. The lowest part of the eastern sky had an almost silvery cast above a slightly orange base. The trees remained massive black forms silhouetted against broad bands of gray sky, but I could pick out more details. I dread for winter to pass.

Near the wood splitter *Mahonia* x *wagneri* 'King's Ransom', a hybrid of *M. pinnata* and *M. aquifolium*, is a shrubby mass of deep burgundy-purple leaves. Its old, leathery leaves have the slightly crackled appearance of an old piano finish and reflect the light as if they were polished. The younger, softer maroon leaves absorb the light like sheared velvet, while those in the interior, untouched by the sun, are still summer green. Racemes of swelling buds at the tips of the branches reveal clusters of overlapping incipient

Fritillaria persica

flowers protected by velvety plum calyxes. Green-flowered hellebores bloom nearby.

Spring rushes forward, winter recedes, and then winter returns and crushes spring. I worry as the seasons overlap and flow into and out of each other. Will our woody plants misjudge the season and release their buds from their protective coverings too soon? Is a mild winter a predictor of a hotter than normal summer? Which plants can survive such inconsistent weather?

Blue *Primula vulgaris* bloomed at Christmas and now, as February ends, the pale yellow wild forms join them. Pink, purple, and near-white flowers appear on plants along the wooded hillside. Most of all I treasure the few self-sown seedlings in the paths. A plant that grows well enough to produce its own seedlings is in the right place.

A bulge in the soil revealed a big, fat, blue-gray-green bud of *Fritillaria persica*. At this stage it looked like an artichoke with outer bracts peeling away from the central cone. Some years the flowers open and occasionally I get seeds, but often a late, severe cold period destroys the buds. It doesn't really matter. This plant is worth growing for this moment alone. Mature growth and opened flowers will be bonuses.

We revised the northeast Color Garden, one of four gardens surrounding the big urn in the sunny gardens. We had talked about it for months, first deciding what was wrong with it last year and then discussing options for improving it. This garden has major contrasts in color and shape. Broad-leaved cannas and zantedeschias accompany slender-leaved *Zephyranthes candida*, black-leaved *Ophiopogon plani-scapus* 'Nigrescens', and small round-leaved callicarpas (beauty berry). The color scheme is black, red, and white. Three white-berried callicarpas, *Calli-carpa japonica* 'Leucocarpa', and near-white *Rosa* 'Nastarana' in the center are underplanted with small divisions of the black-leaved mondo grass from the Circle Garden. Near the edges of the bed we added groups of seedlings from the slender-leaved *Nandina domestica* on the bank and their brilliant red winter foliage transformed the garden the minute we planted them. We imagined the bed as it will be in summer with black-leaved colocasias, near-black dahlias, *Rosa* 'Iceberg', *Lespedeza thunbergii* 'White Fountain', and red-flowered forms of *Salvia greggii*. I wondered whether the reality can be as wonderful as today's vision that includes no insect-eaten plants or mosquito-bitten people, no weeds, no plants out of place. Roger helped with the planting, digging when we dug and pulling at the weeds as we removed them. Bluebirds and white-throated sparrows sang nearby. As the afternoon flew by we heard owls. It was time to close the cold frames.

Stevie, Impy, and Cindy were born on the 24th of February eighteen years ago in Craufurd's study. Craufurd received their mother, Flossie, a handsome, gray, long-haired angora cat, from Steve Lewis at Imparts, his auto repair shop. He thought she was pregnant and the arrival of four kittens shortly after he brought her home confirmed it. 1984 was the first year for Montrose Nursery and she led the kittens along the maze of the foundation of the new, little greenhouse. There will be no party. Cindy seldom gets out of bed. Impy seldom stays still long enough. And Stevie is much too shy.

Japanese apricots, *Prunus mumes*, bloom for most of the month. As soon as I read of this winter-flowering plant in Elizabeth Lawrence's *Gardens in Winter* I began to search for it. After I found one growing in a garden on Anderson Street in Durham, I would go out of my way to drive by it on cold February days. When it died, I mourned as if it were my loss. I finally found and planted one in my first garden, only to leave it when we moved to Hillsborough. Now I have many. Some are named cultivars: darkest pink 'Kobai' and lighter pink 'Peggy Clark'. Others are selections propagated by friends and chance seedlings with single or semi-double flowers in white or shades of pink. I used to think of Japanese apricots as freeze predictors, but now I know that even if weather destroys the earliest flowers, more will open later.

Prunus 'Okame' blooms at the edge of the woods garden with clear pink flowers and yellow stamens on white filaments. Horizontal bands of silver, gray, and beige on its trunk and exfoliating bark in winter are reasons to grow this small tree even if we lose the flowers. Happily all the flowers have not opened, for we are about to experience the coldest temperatures of this winter. How I wish this cold had come in January before the sap rose.

Two mouse cubes set with small bits of Reese's Peanut Butter Cups are on the floor beneath the settle in the law office and every morning I find a mouse in one. I began trapping mice many years ago after hearing them scurrying about this old building when I worked here at night. At first I was terrified at the sight or sound of them but now I think them beautiful, with luxurious coats of tawny brown, large ears, black whiskers, and pink noses and feet. When I carry the traps down to the pond or to a brush pile and turn them upside down, the lid falls open, and the mice scamper out. I wonder whether I keep catching the same one over and over, forcing him to walk up the hill, through the heat duct, out into the room, and back into the little gray box where he has supper and a good night's rest.

Juniperus virginiana that grows by the "dungeon" next to the potting room bloomed late in the month. Golden brown cases filled with pollen lightened the dark green mass of scale-like leaves and the slightest breeze released clouds of yellow pollen.

The dungeon, a small, brick room about a foot below ground, has one window and one door. During the nineteenth century the Grahams kept their food here where it was cooler in summer and warmer in winter. Around

Prunus 'Okame'

Sanguinaria canadensis

1991 we poured a concrete floor and Wayne designed and built sliding shelves for trays to hold seed flats. In this unheated space seeds experience the fluctuating temperatures necessary to induce germination. I had planned to work here away from the rap, rock, or talk radio enjoyed by some of the staff, so we put in a table and hung a fluorescent light above it, but I closed the nursery and reduced the staff before I needed to use the space for potting plants. Mice that like sprouts are our primary pests, so several baited mouse cubes lie in strategic locations about the room.

By the end of February the first bloodroot, *Sanguinaria canadensis*, opened near the metasequoias east of the house where *Cyclamen coum* and *Crocuses vernus* and *tommasinianus* also grow. Other bloodroot flowers remained wrapped in their silvery blue leaves. *Anemone blanda* revealed its blue flowers in mid-day here and along the road to the pond where little bunches of winter aconites, *Eranthis hyemalis*, sown from our seeds, bloomed along with them. I will never have enough aconites or anemones. The first *Trillium pusillum* bloomed in the woods, but when I looked for more in the Rock Garden, I couldn't even find a bulge in the soil.

A large clump of the pure white form of *Calanthe discolor*, a Japanese orchid, grows near the walk in the woods. I dug, divided, and replanted all the pseudobulbs that had growth buds and made a drift of ten or more plants where a few minutes before I had only three and then planted a large flat of back bulbs, that part of the plant below ground which resembles a bulb and remains after the terminal growth has died away. These old pseudobulbs will grow now that they have been separated from their mother bulbs and by next spring I will have twenty or more new plants.

Late in February Bonnie, Cathy, Cheryl, and I went to Big Bloomers, a nursery near Sanford, North Carolina. I was excited when we planned the daylong trip but nearly backed out for I have beds to weed, mulch, and plant. I must pot on more plants to sell at our spring Garden Open Day. I may miss some little event in the garden. We drove along the back roads through the countryside admiring the few remaining undeveloped tracts of land and bemoaning the population increase and the general attitude of most people that undeveloped land is useless land. We saw former forests bare after recent timbering. We arrived at the nursery shortly after ten o'clock and left nearly three hours later. We purchased only one of each cultivar and filled box after box with plants, but only after the reckoning did we wonder whether we could get all the plants plus us back into the car. Most of us held flats on our laps. When we returned, Craufurd asked what we talked about. "Just plants!"

A day looking at new plants stimulated me and I dug with renewed energy while the staff potted *Ajuga pyramidalis* 'Metallica Crispa', *Sarcococca hookeriana* var. *humilis* (sweet box), and *Chrysogonum virginianum* (green-and-gold). We stuck cuttings of some of our new plants and divided dianthus for spring sales. We spread shredded leaves over the Black, White, and Red Garden, and began to cut back and weed the Blue and Yellow one. We pulled out wild onions and oxalis that seem determined to grow everywhere. The onions were here when we came but much oxalis was accidentally planted as we developed this garden. Most potting soil seems to contain oxalis seeds. I cut *Spiraea japonica* 'Limemound' all the way to the ground to reveal the grape hyacinths and crocuses growing nearby and keep the shrub lower in summer. We dug under a cactus, *Opuntia humifusa*, carefully picked up each piece by its root, and removed it from the path.

By the end of February the two largest dawn redwoods, *Metasequoia glyptostroboides*, bloomed. All winter we had watched their brown tassels lengthen as they
dangled from the tips of the branches, but in this final
week the flowers opened and released masses of pollen.
Now a light covering of yellow dust lies over the plants
beneath.

We went from spring back to winter as the month
ended with temperatures in the teens. Hellebores and
arums lay frozen in early morning. They will recover but
Iris unguicularis flowers, that looked perfect when frozen,
defrosted into wilted, blue-purple remnants of their former glory. Although the older tubular, lilac flowers of
Daphne genkwa turned brown, a few young ones with
bright, golden-yellow centers withstood the cold while
at its base a group of winter heaths, *Erica carnea* 'Winter
Beauty', retained its perfect carmine-pink flowers in clusters above dark green needle-like foliage.

Metasequoia glyptostroboides

MARCH

March is spring interrupted by winter. After freezing nights, daffodils lay facedown in the mulch, their stems collapsed at the base. Those with the little protection provided by leafless limbs of nearby trees survived best. *Iris unguicularis* unfolded its buds to form perfect flowers. *Magnolia* x *loebneri* and *Prunus* 'Okame' have limp, brown flowers while *Prunus mume* has perfect pink or white ones. White flowers on the old quince, *Chaenomeles speciosa* 'Nivalis', that was here when we arrived, turned brown but the hybrid, *Chaenomeles* x *superba* 'Crimson and Gold', remained superb with dark red flowers centered with golden anthers. Crocuses can take it. Their flowers looked as if they had never frozen, even though some creature ate their leaves. The little leaf blades will lengthen again next week.

A gentle, steady rain did little to fill the cracks in the soil where we have no grass and the ground looks like it does at the height of summer. We are in the fifth year of a major drought. The lawn is thin and bare except for *Cyclamen coum* and *C. hederifolium*, the former in bloom, the latter in leaf. Such welcome seedlings distract me from the state of the lawn but not from the state of the ground.

Snowdrops are over until fall. It is a long time until October, when they begin to bloom again. Other plants will come into flower but I never forget snowdrop sea-

Prunus mume

son, especially in midsummer when I count the months remaining until they reappear.

Primroses in the woods and bloodroot in the shady gardens proclaim spring. The slightly fuzzy green buds of *Primula sieboldii* along the Mother-in-Law Walk promise flowers, for I have never seen this Japanese primrose injured by cold. Clumps have spread into drifts that form sweeps of white, pink, or purple flowers. Swollen seed capsules of winter aconites mean a good crop of seeds to scratch into the ground if I can collect them at the right moment. I just press them into the soil wherever I want bright yellow flowers in late winter. The flowers on most Christmas roses have turned pink or green as they,

Chaenomeles x *superba* 'Crimson and Gold'

too, ripen their seeds. A few late-blooming forms have fresh, pure white flowers, but this extraordinarily warm winter has brought the entire species along faster than usual. New leaves have already appeared on those recently planted on the wooded hillside.

At dusk wild geese call as they fly in to the pond for the night. Craufurd and I often go down the hill to watch them land with loud splashes and squawks. Sometimes Roger and Tony accompany us. The cats are fascinated by the geese and the geese curious about the cats. Roger is fearless and walks out onto the rickety pier and then down onto a little wooden platform at water level. The geese gather around him in a semicircle as if to hear the news of the day. There is no animosity on either side. The little cat dabbles his paw in the water, and I fully expect him to swim before summer ends. I hope he waits until it is warmer in case I have to dive in to rescue him. Tony keeps his distance, eager to walk back up the hill for dinner, but he turns, looks back, and waits for Roger to catch up with us.

I wish I could read the signs in the woods better. Sometimes I come across areas less than two feet in diameter where an animal must have lain the night before. I find leaves scratched up along the paths and droppings of all sorts. I recognize those from deer and rabbits and I believe I can distinguish fox from dog, but there are many unsolved mysteries. Who bores holes in the lawns and builds tiny nests lined with fur or bits of insulation in the ground? Mole runs are easy—long tunnels that wind through beds, fields, and lawns. The cats are fascinated by them and will sit for hours with heads cocked to one side listening to the moles dig. Alas, their interest is pure curiosity; they seldom catch anything.

Mockingbirds argue over territory in early spring. Two males want to settle into the 'Mary Wallace' rose on the arbor that frames the entrance to the Tropical Garden. They fly at each other, above the arbor, with much cackling and wing flapping. Harsh, rasping sounds replace their beautiful summer songs. Finally the dominant one drives the other away.

Salix babylonica 'Crispa'

The rain left more than an inch of water in our gauge. I can't tell whether it is raining when I first wake up even though I have a green metal standing seam roof outside my bedroom. Two sets of windows between it and me keep out heat, cold, and sounds. I look down on the Dianthus Walk and on good days—that is, rainy days—puddles on the brick path quiver with each new drop.

The first weekend in March I went to the Philadelphia Flower Show. As always, when the time of departure approached, I thought of reasons why I need to stay here, why I shouldn't leave even for a day. Craufurd drove me to the airport early Monday morning. This, my first trip by air since the disaster of 9/11, found me more anxious than usual. I felt I was being dragged away as we left Montrose. The drive, security check, and boarding the small jet were uneventful—almost as it used to be except that there were few people in the airport. The halls were almost empty and my flight had fewer than a dozen passengers. I settled in with a book of short stories by Eudora Welty. Just before takeoff I looked up to see the flight attendant, strapped into his seat facing us. Obviously Middle Eastern, he held both hands near his face as if in prayer. "This is it!" I thought. I knew I shouldn't have come. I sat sadly thinking of my life with Craufurd, took one final mental tour through the garden, thought of each of the cats, and wondered how it would feel to crash into a building. The trip went smoothly. The flight attendant fulfilled his obligations to each of us and settled in to read *A Beautiful Mind*.

I spent the afternoon at the flower show. It was magical. Talented designers put together exhibitions based on the theme Gardening for the Senses. Perfectly grown tropical plants with lush foliage and large containers overflowing with flowers dominated many displays. Plants bloomed together as they never could in gardens. I was most delighted by a hedge of *Salix babylonica* 'Crispa' woven together to form arches with a small-flowered clematis interlaced between the branches. I came away wondering how to go in a different direction. The truth is, I feel uneasy being in style.

Tuesday's judging was delightful because I worked with two intelligent, serious plant people who knew their plants. Our panel worked for about four hours judging many horticulture exhibits, the most difficult being the dwarf conifers. We had to decide whether the small trees were natural dwarfs, young plants, or pruned and starved. These competitions demand great skill from the growers and attention to the tiniest detail. We marveled at clumps of miniature saxifrages, primulas, and small clematises perfectly grown and flowering months ahead of their normal time. We were only pleasantly tired but ready for lunch at the end of duty.

I returned home and felt comforted the minute I walked in the door. All the cats looked up from their beds as if to say, "You back already?" It was a delight to walk down to pick up the morning papers the next morning and see the changes two days made in the garden. In my absence the *Edgeworthia papyrifera* began to bloom near the law office. I could hardly wait to get back to work. We transplanted 'Red Giant' mustard seedlings into individual pots, and weeded the sedum cold frame. We stuck the dangling rosettes of orostachys in gritty soil, cut back sedums, and planned some of our containers for summer.

Edgeworthia papyrifera

Anemone blanda

We discussed the need for contrast, perhaps something tight, green, and cool for our Tropical Garden, where the lush, bold foliage of bananas and cannas combines with the brightly colored flowers of verbenas, cosmos, and marigolds. I had returned inspired.

The gentle, sad cooing of mourning doves summons memories of visits from Craufurd's parents when we lived in Durham and of the bird we saved shortly after moving to Hillsborough, when a dove struck a window at the back of the house and fell, stunned, to the ground. We put it into a cat carrier, and placed the container in the pit below the law office, where we fed it moistened cat food and water. Several days later, when we opened the cage, it flew away. We believe the dove that flew to us and landed at our feet many times during that summer was the same one.

The second week in March more *Anemones blanda*, wind flowers, bloomed near the large metasequoias. From about a dozen dark gray tubers planted when I began that garden, hundreds have spread up the slope and over to the path. The anemones were supposed to have blue flowers but many have petals shaded from blue to near white, and a few are all white. They intermingle with the gracefully twisting foliage of foxy-scented starflowers, *Ipheion uniflorum*. Forms with white flowers have bluish leaves and those with blue flowers have greenish ones.

Ipheion uniflorum

Euphorbia x *martini*

An underplanting of yellow creeping jenny, *Lysimachia nummularia* 'Aurea', and hundreds of self-sown seedlings of *Euphorbia* x *martini* tie it all together.

The silver- or pewter-leaved *Cyclamen coum* near here have predominantly pink flowers. Some are shaded and others are nearly white with just a hint of pink at the base of the petals. A few have petals that spread out from the base and never fold back in typical cyclamen fashion. Dark, crinkled, near-black leaves of *Ajuga pyramidalis* 'Metallica Crispa' provide the perfect background for the cyclamen. *Isopyrum biternatum*, at the top of the mound between the metasequoias, quivers in every breeze. With leaves like columbine, and flowers like rue anemone, this shade-loving native plant delights us from late fall when it begins to grow until early summer when it disappears underground. We usually have at least one flower open by Christmas and masses by the end of February and early March.

Isopyrum biternatum

Trillium cuneatum

The sessile species (including *Trillium cuneatum*) and forms of trilliums that grow in this garden show their green leaves mottled with silver and brown surrounding young buds that will open before April. The leaves form a platform for flat green sepals and erect yellow or dark maroon flowers. Jack-in-the-Green forms of *Primula vulgaris* have opened a few, pale yellow flowers with ruffled green collars by early March and will continue to bloom for nearly two months. Pulmonarias now have pink buds and a few blue flowers. The brilliant yellow, hoop-skirt-like flowers of *Narcissus bulbocodium* bloom with tiny vestigial petals and flaring cups while not far away clusters of small, pale pink flowers of a squill, *Scilla bifolia* 'Rosea', are about to burst out of their protective calyxes.

Primula vulgaris Jack-in-the-Green

The two large, pyramidal metasequoias, that give this garden its name, grow on mounds that dry out in summer. When I planted the ground beneath them in 1993, I didn't know whether I could garden here, for their spreading roots are large and shallow, but they are good hosts and provide much needed shade in summer and full sun in winter when the plants beneath them are in growth.

I developed many friendships by mail during the nursery years. These correspondences were usually stimulated, at least in the beginning, by our common interest in a specific plant or season. Dr. David Gurin, from Long Island, wrote me of his love of winter-blooming plants, so I sent him a piece of *Adonis* 'Fukujukai' one fall. He seemed grateful but nothing he said could have prepared me for the box of double white *Trillium grandiflorum* he sent the following spring. Where could I grow them? I had no bed prepared. We planted them in good soil beneath the large trees near the driveway where we knew we would see every flower. Years later we added cyclamen and edged the drive with the same tiny mondo grass, *Ophiopogon japonicus*, that I used this winter in the new Snowdrop Walk.

Shortly after I closed the nursery, I expanded this narrow strip along the driveway to include metasequoias. The city brought ground-up leaves, which we spread thickly over the skimpy lawn, and I began to plant cyclamen formerly used as seed parents for the nursery, trilliums, bloodroot, and dentaria from Mother's garden, and special hellebores. Hostas, primroses, phloxes, pulmonarias, and epimediums went in next, and then I waited anxiously to see what survived. The hostas were the only failures, not because of their location, but because they are a favorite food of our deer. Two years later the plants in this garden began to flow together.

As March progressed, darkest purple-flowered *Crocus tommasinianus* yielded to *C. vernus*, the last crocus of the season, and the brilliant crimson flowers of *Cyclamen pseudibericum* overlapped those of *C. coum* and

Cyclamen pseudibericum

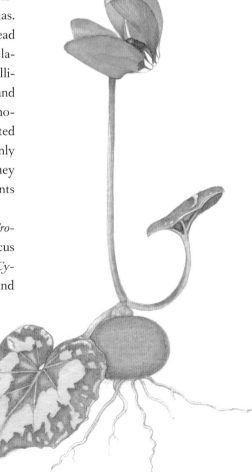

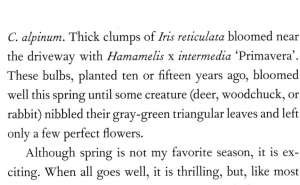

Iris reticulata

C. alpinum. Thick clumps of *Iris reticulata* bloomed near the driveway with *Hamamelis* x *intermedia* 'Primavera'. These bulbs, planted ten or fifteen years ago, bloomed well this spring until some creature (deer, woodchuck, or rabbit) nibbled their gray-green triangular leaves and left only a few perfect flowers.

Although spring is not my favorite season, it is exciting. When all goes well, it is thrilling, but, like most thrills, it also contains disappointments. Buds that promise beauty of color or shape may open, followed by unseasonably cold temperatures that destroy flowers. In a good spring several species of winter hazels, corylopsis, bloom for weeks. *C. pauciflora*, near the large yew, bears chartreuse flowers that tumble out of their reddish brown calyxes. The entire shrub looks ready to implode into a gentle shower of clusters of small flowers suspended in time and space. Will they open? New bright yellow leaves of periwinkle, *Vinca minor* 'Alba Variegata', cover the ground beneath this shrub.

Low-lying morning mists linger at this season and we often hear bagpipes in the distance. This must be the sight and sound that Scottish settlers left when they moved from Scotland to central North Carolina. In the cool, damp air we see shapes of trees but few details. A mockingbird sings every tune in his repertoire. Bluebirds warble their sweet songs and cardinals sing their liquid

Corylopsis pauciflora

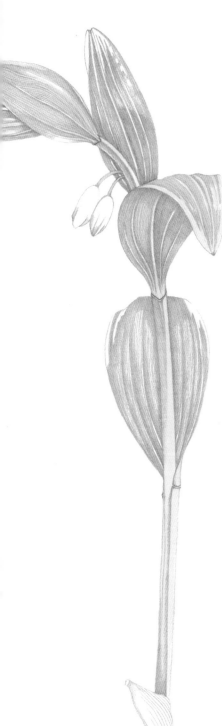

tunes. In the potting room we prepared plants for Garden Open Day in April. We chopped up the rhizomes of Solomon's seal, *Polygonatum odoratum* 'Variegatum', divided tricyrtis, potted up rooted cuttings of some of our favorite barberries, and cleaned up and potted on *Isopyrum biternatum*.

We learned why the bagpiper was practicing. Elizabeth "Boo" Collins died at age ninety. She was one of the last descendents of the Scots who settled this town. We attended her funeral service at St. Matthew's Episcopal Church nearby and, after the tolling of the bell, went with the family into the cemetery accompanied by the music of the bagpiper. St. Matthew's is one of the oldest churches in Hillsborough. Many Grahams, including Sandy, from whom, with his brother, we purchased this property, and his father and mother, from whom he inherited it, are buried on the church grounds. When we first moved here, we saw the Graham monument easily from the lawn west of the house and felt as if they watched to see what the new people would do to their property. But now trees and shrubs impede our view. Perhaps they have accepted us.

Warm days followed by warm nights brought spring forward. Starry white bloodroot, *Sanguinaria canadensis*, stand out against the freshly fallen, cinnamon-colored mulch of spent dawn redwood flowers. Although most bloodroot flowers are single, we also grow a few semi-double forms with round petals and others with more pointed and widely separated ones. That weedy, annual cress, *Cardamine hirsuta*, that seeds so abundantly, sur-

Polygonatum odoratum 'Variegatum'

rounds them. With thumb at a right angle to the ground and forefinger pressed against the base of each rosette, I pull out each little plant easily. The race between rapidly ripening seed capsules and me is perennial. I know I will never win.

Lysimachia nummularia 'Aurea' grows brighter each day. Although the leaves in winter had chartreuse undertones to their brownish bronze color, now they begin to glow. Creeping jenny brings attention first to itself and then to everything growing with it. Black mondo grass (*Ophiopogon planiscapus* 'Nigrescens'), white starflowers, black violas, black-leaved *Ranunculus ficaria* 'Brazen Hussy', *Euphorbia* x *martini*, and *Anemone blanda* all show up against this yellow-green carpet. It unifies the garden.

I removed the old beige blades of *Hakonechloa macra* 'Aureola' to reveal their new bright green and yellow shoots. Most of my shady gardens are too dry for this, one of the most elegant grasses, so I grow it successfully in an iron pot near the house where we water it well in summer. Curving masses of variegated leaves hover over the pot by summer's end.

As the month progresses flowers appear on redbuds, cherries, and the deliciously fragrant clove currant, *Ribes odoratum*, a present many years ago from Allen Lacy.

Ribes odoratum

Bright yellow calyxes obscure small petals — sometimes red, sometimes yellow — that form a cup nestled at the base of each flower of this shrub. Behind the smokehouse, in part sun, the currant has spread into many shrubby clumps. The smokehouse, a small building southeast of the law office, retains the smoky stains from its former use. Originally it had a dirt floor, but after the Grahams stopped smoking meats, they put in a wood floor and young John Graham used it as his clubhouse. John decided he needed a window from which to see anyone who approached the building, so he cut a hole in the door. His father, Alexander H. Graham, was horrified when he discovered this mutilation, but later agreed that to be useful the window needed to open and close, so he installed a track in which to slide the wood removed from the door. A semi-detached set of privies remains behind the smokehouse. Steps lead to a little covered area where previous generations of Grahams waited their turns. The east side, the women's room, has three holes, two for adults, and one for a child. We store hoses in this room. The west side, for men, has only two holes. We store containers of nursery pots on the bench in this room. The initials JAG remain where they were carved near the door to the "sitting room." James Alexander Graham must have had a long wait!

When Craufurd and I arrived at Montrose, we put brush and tree limbs into places we thought might erode. We had filled in an eroded gully behind our house in Durham during our fourteen years there and, before we left, had stabilized the area enough to plant trees. This approach solves several problems. We get rid of the brush, provide a habitat for other creatures living on the property, and eventually have another area suitable for planting. Early this spring we cleared away the remnants of an old brush pile in the woods garden. We moved old fence posts, rotting steps, bits of rotting clapboards, old bricks and mortar, as well as many of the fallen branches we had thrown into it. Much of the original debris had decayed into velvety soil, but we

threw that which remained intact into another low area. We dug out tree seedlings and a large patch of that pesky *Lamium galeobdolon*, brought in accidentally with bags of leaves.

After mulching the banks and lower area with about nine inches of shredded leaves, we laid out a new path to the Mother-in-Law Walk and covered it with wood chips. Uncovered earth is an invitation to chaos. Suddenly this section became a canvas waiting for paint. But longer days, warmer temperatures, and rain meant we must go back to the sunny gardens to finish spring cleaning and planting. The canvas had to remain bare.

Several old junipers grow on the terrace below the barnyard in a diagonal line, which, if the planting were extended, would meet at a magnificent tulip poplar, *Liriodendron tulipifera*, east of the newly cleared Basin. The diagonal emphasizes the perspective and makes the tree seem even larger and more distant than it is. A self-sown holly, *Ilex opaca*, and *Magnolia macrophylla* had grown tall enough to spoil our view so I cut them down. This was a painful decision, for I had watched the little holly grow and it turned out to be a female with its first berries, and the magnolia, planted in error, was finally large enough to bloom. I had to do it. At last I have regained my unencumbered view.

We live next to Cameron Park Elementary School, where the happy sounds of children at play accompany our work. During late winter Craufurd and I found balloons with notes attached in bushes and in the field between the school and us. Each note contained the same message written in a different hand. The students in the second grade released one hundred balloons on the one-hundredth day of school and they wanted to know when and where their balloons were found. I answered each note as we found it, and received replies. The students were clearly disappointed to learn that the balloons traveled only to the next property. They told me of their favorite subjects, invited me to their houses, asked whether I gardened in a dress, and sent a painting of two people with two cats.

Liriodendron tulipifera and *Juniperus virginiana*

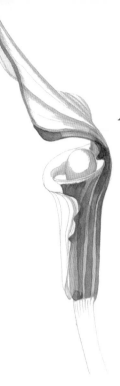

Arisaema sikokianum

Magnolias turned to mush again after a temperature in the low twenties. I hadn't covered any plant and feared destruction in every section of the garden. Most aroids can't take this, and I had *Arisaema sazensoo* and *A. sikokianum*, relatives of our native jack-in-the-pulpits, fully open. *Primula kisoana*, with bright pink flowers on pink hairy stalks, was at a vulnerable stage. How I wish I could be in charge of weather. I wish we could have just one gentle spring with slowly increasing temperatures and none of the violent fluctuations that lead plants into growth too soon.

Late this month we let Stevie go out at her own request and that was the last we saw of her. A beautiful little charcoal tabby with white paws and a white bib, she was eighteen years and one month old. Stevie was an unusually shy creature, ill at ease with strangers, easily spooked, but very affectionate. In the mornings she would sit next to Craufurd on the bench at our breakfast table and demand hugs and each evening she sat on my lap for a brief period of mutual declarations of affection. We put a little headstone and marker in our cat cemetery even though we have no body to bury.

Amorphophallus konjac, devil's tongue, finally bloomed. Each spring for more than five years it produced one divided leaf on a stalk mottled with burgundy, gray, and green about fifteen inches high. Although I put the tuber in a larger pot each year it burst each one by the end of summer. Every fall I brought in the tuber, with its leaf withering away, and stored it dry on the gravel in the little greenhouse. In February this year I saw the tip of a burgundy-brown triangle, the first sign of a bloom. We watched it daily and at last have a thick flower stalk marked with gray and olive green and the tip of a spadix protruding above its wavy cloak of a spathe. I expect it to stink when it opens fully, but until that moment enjoy watching this curious flower develop.

Mornings are filled with a cacophony of sounds. Every bird declares itself with cackling, whistling, or warbling. Hearing them is like listening to a complex fugue. At first I enjoy the combination of sounds but later want to separate them and focus on each musical line. Towhees seem to set the key and tempo. Bluebirds and cardinals sing all day as they go to their nests in wooden birdhouses or in the midst of shrubs. I recognize a few bird sounds but wish my father were here to identify the others for me. He knew most local birds by sight, flight, and sound and used to tell me which bird we heard, but I paid little attention.

Primula kisoana

He knew which stayed here for the winter and where the others went when they left. I need another lesson.

Bonnie, Cathy, Cheryl, and I tackled the large sugarcane relative, *Saccharum arundinaceum*, in the Blue and Yellow Garden this week. All winter we enjoyed the music made by the wind rustling its leaves but new growth at the base led us to cut away last year's growth. Each worked from a different edge cutting and tossing the old stalks over the fence. We met in the middle and hauled the debris to the brush pile laughing and singing "Whistle While You Work." I repeated my parents' saying that used to make my brother, sister, and me groan: "When we all work, it's fun!"

We pruned the yellow-leaved willow, shaping the tree to let light and air into its center, and cut away dead branches from the ring of boxwoods, *Buxus sempervirens* 'Suffruticosa', in the Blue and Yellow Garden. All month we cut down grasses and cleaned up shrubs including removing the dense growth at the base of *Ligustrum* 'Vicaryi', one of the most important plants in the sunny gardens. Its chartreuse leaves in summer intensify the brilliant colors in our Bright Color Garden, and relieve the somber brick-red and purple of the tiles on the sides of the garage. They echo the yellow of the Blue and Yellow Garden and form a transition to other sunny gardens linking one bed to another. They focus our attention on the Albert Memorial, an elaborate urn, at the western end of the vista seen through the lath house.

In late March we work until the light fades, replacing dead plants with new ones. I never put anything into the ground without imagining what form, color, and texture it will add to a bed. Young plants wait in the cold frames for clear signs that spring is here. The terrible freeze last April meant I had to replant, but with only a few extra calendulas and California poppies this year I must get the timing right.

Owls sing at all times of the day accompanied by screaming crows trying without success to drive them away. When we closed the cold frames late one afternoon, we heard the owl's long, gurgling song interrupted by another nearby owl. They sang a splendid duet almost like the evening sounds of kookaburras in Australia. When we followed their sound to a group of old junipers behind Nandinaland, a large owl flew silently away. We looked up and saw an enormous nest in one of the trees and down to see bird droppings at the base of the tree. We had found the barred owl's nest. I hoped, in vain, to see a young owl peering over the side.

We cut the multi-stemmed dogwoods down to about twelve inches in Nandinaland and the Circle Garden in late March. This is like changing the set on a stage. The shape of the bed remains as it was but the interior is transformed not by what we add but by what we subtract. We pruned *Cornus sanguinea* 'Winter Beauty' and *C. sericea* 'Flaviramea' down to about a foot above ground. I do this radical pruning when the brilliant coral color begins to fade from *C. s.* 'Winter Beauty', knowing that these dogwoods must be cut early enough to make substantial growth in summer. After the operation, the gardens look better. Now *Chamaecyparis obtusa* 'Limerick' seems brighter and the grafted plant from our deodara cedar's witch's broom, a mound of medium-green needles, is more visible.

We created Nandinaland about fifteen years ago. When Craufurd and I moved here, we came to a property with fences that separated many areas. A chain link fence extended south from St. Marys Road to the machine shed near the barn. Every winter I removed weeds and vines that covered sections of that fence only to leave an ugly expanse of steel wire, so we gave it to the man who removed it. Birds had inadvertently planted a line of small shrubs, including nandinas and mahonias bound together by miles of honeysuckle, in the shade of a large ash. We moved the nandinas to form a crescent in front of two large eastern red cedars, *Juniperus virginiana*, and dug out most of the honeysuckle. After truckloads of mulch smothered the grass, we planted *Helleborus foetidus*, the early flowering *Narcissus* 'Rijnveld's Early Sensation', and Paul's brightly colored chamaecyparis. We added a young winter sweet, *Chimonanthus praecox* var. *luteus*, now a large shrub, and a gracefully pendulous young youpon holly, *Ilex vomitoria* 'Folsom's Weeping'. During later years we added more plants selected primarily for winter interest. The name "Nandinaland" originated with Ruth Batchelor, who helped us during the nursery years. She was our quality control. She made certain each plant on the order form was checked, double checked the addresses on the mailing label and order form, and sealed and weighed each box. After shipping season, she became a weeder but it was usually early summer by the time she could get to the garden and the weeds were often higher than she was. After searching the property for her one day, I finally found her in the midst of the microstegium in this garden where she replied, "Here I am — in Nandinaland."

APRIL

This is the busiest month of the year for tours, the garden, and the Montrose Nursery. We must prepare for two Garden Mornings, when we will share our knowledge of plants, design, and techniques of propagation with those who want to know how we manage this garden. This year we will focus on the recently restored Dianthus Walk. The screenings spread in early February did what we hoped they would and now more plants have produced tufts of new foliage above the grit. Johnny-jump-ups and *Phlox subulata* are already in bloom and dianthuses in bud. During the Garden Morning we will show how we divide bulbs and epimediums, sow seeds, and take and stick cuttings of woody and herbaceous plants. We will present a collection of gift plants to each person as a reminder of this day. Our greatest challenge is to teach something useful and interesting to those who have attended most of our workshops.

The other major spring event, Garden Open Day, is one of two annual events when we close the gates partially and open the garden to the public. Guests park at Cameron Park Elementary School next door because our narrow driveway allows only a single lane of traffic. Worried about the impact of large numbers of visitors on the land, I rarely advertise this day but send notices to those on the mailing list and hand out announcements to others we think may be interested.

At this season we divide our workdays into three sections. First we go to the nursery area and collect plants for dividing or repotting. Each of us brings up to the potting room all of one species to prepare for sale and then we work together on one section of the garden. We weed, prune, and mulch the sunny gardens and in early afternoon return to the potting room to deal with the plants we brought up. At the end of each day the finished plants go back to the sales area. Diverse tasks mean we aren't exhausted at the end of the day and no area is completely neglected.

As the weather warms we give more tours and I have an excuse to wander leisurely through the garden with interesting and interested people. I look for faults, not in the visitors, but in my garden. I try to imagine each bed as if I were a visitor seeing it for the first time and see weeds, dead branches, and bits of paper and other debris that came in with the mulch. At the end of most tours another area is added to our "Must Be Weeded Now" or "Should Have Been Weeded Yesterday" lists. But I also usually find new plants in growth or flower that I might otherwise have missed.

Aroids, including *Arisaema sikokianum*, *A. ringens*, and our native jack-in-the-pulpit, *A. triphyllum*, are blooming almost three weeks earlier than usual. Japanese primroses, *Primula sieboldii*, have nearly reached their peak along the south side of the Mother-in-Law Walk where their flowers remain fresh and crisp even after unusually hot spells of eighty degrees or more in early April. This primrose spreads slowly underground and now, fifteen years after planting them, large drifts of each form mingle with their neighbors, their colors blending perfectly without a hint of dissonance. Another Japanese primula, bright pink-flowered *P. kisoana*, is also at its best in several parts in the shady gardens. Hundreds of minute white and pink hairs cover the bloom stalks that rise above softly mounding rosettes of leaves. Plants creep out of the beds into the paths, preferring wood chips to dirt. They can grow anywhere they will in this garden.

Trillium grandiflorum blooms at the edge of the woods. This, the most beautiful species, is always later than most sessile-flowered species. I hope the deer leave it alone this year. They have eaten most *T. pusillum* and are munching their way through the Metasequoia Garden. I can't hate the deer; I hate what we are doing to their habitat, forcing more and more animals onto less and less land. I only wish I could persuade them to stay out of my garden or to graze on the lawn and in the wild places near the river. Across the path from the trilliums the delicate flowers of *Jeffersonia diphylla*, twinleaf, appear to float above the ground. I have grown the Japanese species, *J. dubia*, successfully for years, but finally established our native one only after adding lime to the soil.

Amorphophallus had to leave the greenhouse early in the month. When the flower opened, the odor permeated the entire building. Rotten fish? Perhaps, but that didn't deter us from going several times a day to see its extraordinary bloom. The dark maroon spadix rose above the spathe, and the spathe, which had been tightly wound around it, curled back like an elegant cape with ruffled edges. It goes into the shade of a viburnum for the day, but into the warmer garage for protection at night.

Amorphophallus konjac

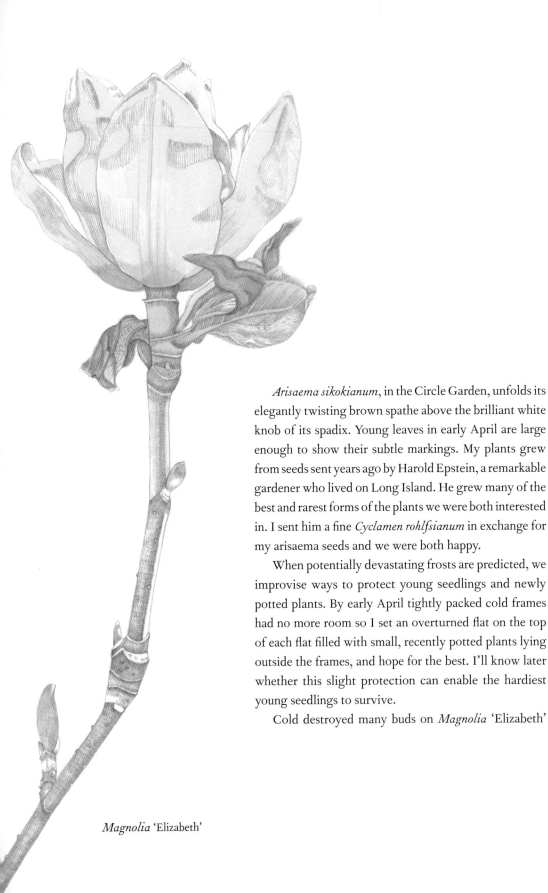

Arisaema sikokianum, in the Circle Garden, unfolds its elegantly twisting brown spathe above the brilliant white knob of its spadix. Young leaves in early April are large enough to show their subtle markings. My plants grew from seeds sent years ago by Harold Epstein, a remarkable gardener who lived on Long Island. He grew many of the best and rarest forms of the plants we were both interested in. I sent him a fine *Cyclamen rohlfsianum* in exchange for my arisaema seeds and we were both happy.

When potentially devastating frosts are predicted, we improvise ways to protect young seedlings and newly potted plants. By early April tightly packed cold frames had no more room so I set an overturned flat on the top of each flat filled with small, recently potted plants lying outside the frames, and hope for the best. I'll know later whether this slight protection can enable the hardiest young seedlings to survive.

Cold destroyed many buds on *Magnolia* 'Elizabeth'

Magnolia 'Elizabeth'

but those that survived opened their pale yellow flowers
at the branch tips in mid-April. The silky, furry gray buds
on *Magnolia macrophylla* remain tightly closed. I grew
this tree from a seed obtained from the American Horticultural Society in 1969. I was a new gardener then,
living in Durham and developing my first garden, and
I was curious about all plants. I wanted to grow everything and concentrated first on woody plants, especially
hollies, stewartias, and viburnums. When we moved to
Hillsborough in 1977, most plants stayed in my old garden but I couldn't leave this magnolia. It was eight years
old and hadn't bloomed, so I dug and transplanted it in
August—not a recommended time. I planted it in the best
place I could find, full sun at the edge of the driveway.
If I had done a little research, I would have discovered
that this magnolia prefers shade. The tree barely existed
for two years, but finally took hold and has grown into a
magnificent specimen. It looks a little stressed by the end

Magnolia macrophylla in bud

Magnolia macrophylla

of our hot summers, but blooms better than any I have since planted in shade.

Most days I catch a mouse so I called Ippy at seven one morning to come and draw him. He looked like the others I have trapped, but it is difficult for me, a human, to distinguish one mouse from another. He is handsome with a thick coat of caramel-colored fur, a white belly, and large round ears, not so large as Mickey Mouse's, but larger than those of the mice that used to terrify my mother. Ippy arrived early and we took the mouse in his little box into the restored kitchen we now call Ippy's room. By mid-morning she had finished his portrait and we took him to the brush pile to release him. He behaved as he has in the past. As we passed the big greenhouse, he became very active and began to wash his face. We turned from the road into the woods toward the brush pile, and he became extremely agitated running back and forth in his box. When we finally reached the pile he was scratching in anticipation of his release but when I turned the box over, he was so excited he wouldn't go to the back so the little door could open. We finally worked it out, and he ran quickly out of the cage into the same opening in the pile he has entered every day I've caught him (or his twin).

There is an almost indescribable joy every afternoon when we get into the garden to weed. I always feel a release of tension, a thrill when my hands and knees reach the soil, and satisfaction when I pull a weed up by the roots. The tearing sound of roots coming away from their earthy home provides a subtle but ever present undertone to the music of the garden. The air is crisp and clear — we have more threatened returns to winter. We didn't finish. We never finish. I hope I never ever finish.

Nature does not allow absolute perfection in a garden so winter returned as predicted. Because of this spring's many commitments I decided to try to protect my most precious, vulnerable plants and carried large pots and buckets to the garden to decide what to save and what to abandon. I want seeds on *Arisaemas sikokianum*, so I covered those. *Primula kisoana* is at its peak, so I covered the ones in the Metasequoia Garden. I covered bananas that were about a foot tall, and the lespedezas we had just cut down. Our temperature went to nearly twenty-five degrees and the results were surprising. Beneath the buckets I found some perfect arisaema flowers, and some shriveled up ones a foot away. Primulas look perfect, but most lespedezas and bananas were damaged.

Reluctantly we turned our clocks ahead the first Saturday night in April and I moved back two months in time. Again the trees become black silhouettes against

gray sky in early morning. Silvery gray and creamy yellow show up in the Dianthus Walk and Circle Garden, but green disappears. The extra light at the end of the day is of little use to me.

When Craufurd returned from Duke one evening, he said there was a large white object at the pond. We used to catch poachers down there but find fewer and fewer now that the word has spread. We call the sheriff's office whenever we see uninvited guests. We went along the road to the pond talking and walking softly, almost silently, and along the way he acknowledged that it might just be a precocious dogwood tree in bloom. At the dam face we looked north and saw a very large white heron. Suddenly a great blue heron and a smaller one flew into the trees on the east side of the pond. There were geese near us and ducks at the north end so we looked and left them as they were. We were the intruders.

The Metasequoia Garden at its peak in mid-April is thrilling, for this garden has grown beyond me. Although I selected the plants to grow here at its beginning, they settled in and spread throughout the entire area. I planted only purple *Phlox divaricata*, but now we have assorted shaped flowers in white, pink, and shades of purple and blue. Species primroses, *Primula elatior*, bloom at the base of the large planting of isopyrums. This is a garden of my dreams, but not of my making. I could never have created such a natural intermingling of plants by planting them individually; it had to come from within — a random self-sowing of seeds.

The day before the first Garden Morning we rehearsed our presentations. Although we won't give a garden tour, we will concentrate on the Metasequoia Garden and Dianthus Walk and I hope each person will leave with a new idea about something, whether design, plant production, or maintenance doesn't matter. Both days were cold and wet but we thought they were successful. We had no choice about sitting in the rain for the discussion of the Dianthus Walk and for the division of corydalis tubers, but everyone enjoyed the time in the warmer potting room best. As always, we learned from our visitors while they learned from us. An owl flew silently across the

Phlox divaricata

Circle Garden near where we sat and later in the morning he sang and his partner answered. They were our cheerleaders.

Summer intruded into spring during the third week of April with temperatures during the day around ninety degrees and those at night around seventy. Primroses wilted and the leaves on most cyclamen began to turn yellow as they went into dormancy earlier than usual. I am tempted to feel cheated out of spring, a little sorry for myself, and very sorry for the plants until I remember we had spring all winter.

We prepared for Garden Open Day. In the past we cut the old stalks of half-hardy salvias, artemisias, buddlejas, agastaches, and verbenas as we mulched each bed in winter and many plants died. This year I waited until late spring to do it and found strong, vigorous growth beneath their twiggy blankets. I will prune again at this time, despite the messy winter look and frantic cleanup as late spring warms toward summer.

Several new peonies bloomed this year but unseasonable heat meant that each flower lasted only a day. *Paeonia broteroi* in the Circle Garden produced two medium pink flowers with crepey petals turned up to form shallow cups. White-flowered *P. daurica*, now *P. mascula* subsp. *triternata*, had a similar shape and nearly transparent petals while the most beautiful of all, *P. obovata*, bore white flowers with a dark crimson tip to the stigma. My tree peony,

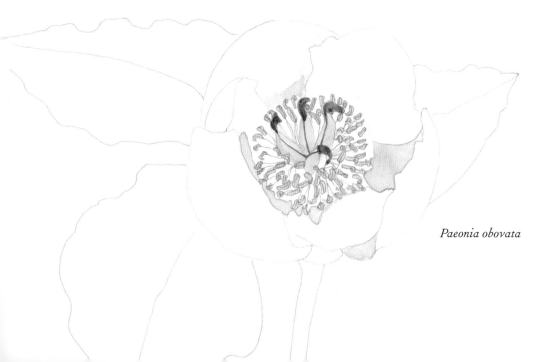

Paeonia obovata

Epimedium grandiflorum 'Koji'

P. suffruticosa, seemed better able to withstand the heat and bloomed with double pink flowers marked with dark burgundy toward the center. I grew all these plants from seed many years ago, planted most in high shade, but put a few in dense shade in the woods. The flowers were worth the wait. Now that they have reached blooming age, I hope for more flowers each year and eventually seeds.

Epimediums bloom in all the wooded areas with flowers in shades of yellow, pink, mauve, and white on slender stalks above their leaves. I have purchased as many as I can find reasonably priced in catalogs and cherish the chance seedlings that appear in every bed. A clear pink seedling—identical except for color—grows near the white *E.* x *setosum*. I would hate to have to choose a favorite but like especially tiny *E. diphyllum* with white flowers and the larger *E. grandiflorum* 'Koji' with violet ones. Dramatic *E. acuminatum* with lilac sepals and dark violet petals and nectaries forces me to turn up the flowering stalk to see both colors. It is an incentive to weed nearby.

The first bloom on summer-flowering *Cyclamen purpurascens* looks fresh with fragrant, bright magenta petals flung back from the mouth of the flower. Now that it appeared, I will have one or more every day until mid-fall. That is the joy of the garden. Just when I feel sad at the end of one plant's season, I feel excitement at the beginning of another's. Many half-hardy salvias are back in growth. Tender *Tweedia caerulea* has a promising shoot at its base and a few plants of the sugar cane, *Saccharum officinarum* 'Pele's Smoke', show signs of life in the May Garden.

Many groups visit the garden at this season. These tours remind people that we are here, bring in some of the income necessary for salaries and plants, and keep us on our toes. All of us study the plants in each garden and learn, relearn, or relearn again their names. We talk about the many ways we might pronounce botanical names and keep the garden as neat and welltended as possible. Most visitors are well-behaved and we enjoy meeting them unless we get behind in our weeding or the weather turns unusually hot. Then we feel the stress.

Premature summer yielded to spring with another threatened frost but brought the cool, clear air that intensifies colors, scents, and shapes of the garden. We replanted calendulas and poppies that didn't survive the heat and cut down more old growth that had protected half-hardy perennials. We cleared the paths of excess verbenas and larkspur but left large groups of poppies wherever they appeared.

A group from the Garden Conservancy came to talk about the future of the gardens at Montrose. They were encouraging about the garden itself and sympathetic to our wish to ensure its survival. We have no desire to freeze the garden in time but believe the best use for this land is to have gardens around the house and upper terraces and wilderness throughout the flood plain. We want to retain the feeling of the old place and keep the formal layout of the kitchen garden as it was in the nineteenth century, but plant it exuberantly. The terraces must remain as they were shaped in the 1930s but the plantings there should be informal with drifts of naturalized native and exotic plants. Bill Noble, Marco Polo Stufano, and Patti McGee walked with us through all the gardens and listened to our hopes and plans. At the end of the day I felt more optimistic about the long-term future of this place than ever before.

After they left we set up the sales benches in preparation for Garden Open Day later that week. We selected and arranged plants from our cold frames and greenhouses. The weather forecast is encouraging — a cloudy day in the mid-seventies — which, if we have a little rain before, will be perfect.

Leafy trees darkened the woods so that I no longer see the terraces below the gardens. Dense, protective shade keeps the soil cooler but drier than that in sun. Straw-colored winter aconites, *Eranthis hyemalis*, have collapsed, galanthus leaves lie on the ground, and the seeds of many crocuses have risen above the soil ready for dispersal. Hellebore seeds ripened and, although I collected many produced by hand pollination, I didn't get all of them.

Vegetables grew in the garden south of the law office when Craufurd and I moved here. A cedar post-and-wire fence surrounded it with two entrances on the north side near the law office. *Rosa* 'Mary Wallace' grew at one entrance and *R.* 'Doctor W. Van Fleet' at the other and they grow near there still. The entire area was laid out in three main sections going from north to south. Each section was sixty feet wide and about one hundred and eighty feet long. Raised grass paths separated and further divided these rectangular strips and an arbor supporting scuppernong grapes dominated the center of the entire garden.

By late April the main sunny borders in this, the former kitchen garden, grow brighter each day. New burgundy leaves on our best smoke tree, *Cotinus coggygria* 'Royal Purple', and the smoky burgundy leaves of *Berberis* x *ottawensis* appear darker than usual against their bright yellow flowers.

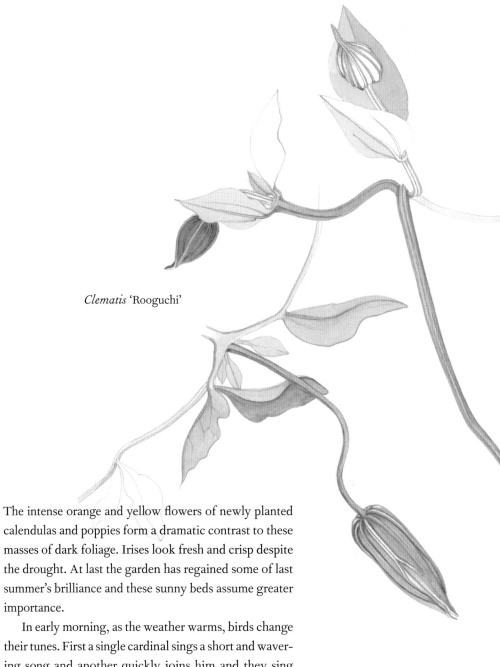

Clematis 'Rooguchi'

The intense orange and yellow flowers of newly planted calendulas and poppies form a dramatic contrast to these masses of dark foliage. Irises look fresh and crisp despite the drought. At last the garden has regained some of last summer's brilliance and these sunny beds assume greater importance.

In early morning, as the weather warms, birds change their tunes. First a single cardinal sings a short and wavering song and another quickly joins him and they sing trills, each overlapping the other, and each in his own key.

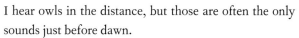

I hear owls in the distance, but those are often the only sounds just before dawn.

Garden Open Day this year was our most successful public event yet with a steady stream of visitors. Those who came early went immediately to the plant sale and then to the garden, and some newcomers who came late had learned of it from friends during the day. Sales were good and we had little trouble with plant snatchers or people who wanted to go into the woods and other forbidden areas. A few seedlings in the paths were trampled but the gardens themselves were untouched. Craufurd was treasurer, so we didn't have to calculate or handle the money. Our friends and neighbors Marsha Ferree and Maureen Quilligan welcomed people as they came into the garden. Marsha counted the visitors by putting a bean from one pocket into the other as each person came up the drive. Clouds kept the temperature low enough for comfort and the light was perfect for photographers.

The clematises in bloom inspired more questions than any other plants. Our deer have not yet discovered our best forms of *Clematis integrifolia* this year so their large twisted bells of medium gray-blue or pink hang down on stalks about fifteen inches above the mulch. The large white stars of *C. patens* face outward on vines clinging to the stiff stems of *Rosa* 'Mermaid', and red *C. texensis* blooms on the west side of the lath house and through the January jasmine along the driveway. In the May Garden a dark, indigo blue, campanulate clematis, *C.* 'Rooguchi', clambers through a buddleja.

Halesia carolina

As spring progresses delicate white bell-like flowers hang from *Halesia carolina*, silverbell tree, that grows between two compost piles where it provides reason enough to volunteer to carry down the spent nursery soil and kitchen leavings. Fresh young leaves accompany the remaining clusters of three or more pendulous, fragrant flowers. At the edge of the woods the shiny leaves of a late-flowering *Arisaema ringens* protect the snail-like flower. Its spathe, striped with soft green and delicate brown covers a chocolate-burgundy curl. Fragrant flowers of the fringe tree, *Chionanthus virginicus*, perfume the front garden. Our one plant, about twelve feet tall, grows near the metasequoias where we found it when we arrived. By the end of April clusters of dangling, thread-like, white petals look like white smoke surrounding the tree.

A drift of *Trillium catesbyi* with elegantly twisting, medium pink petals grows on the slope in the woods. I increased this plant years ago by uncov-

Trillium catesbyi

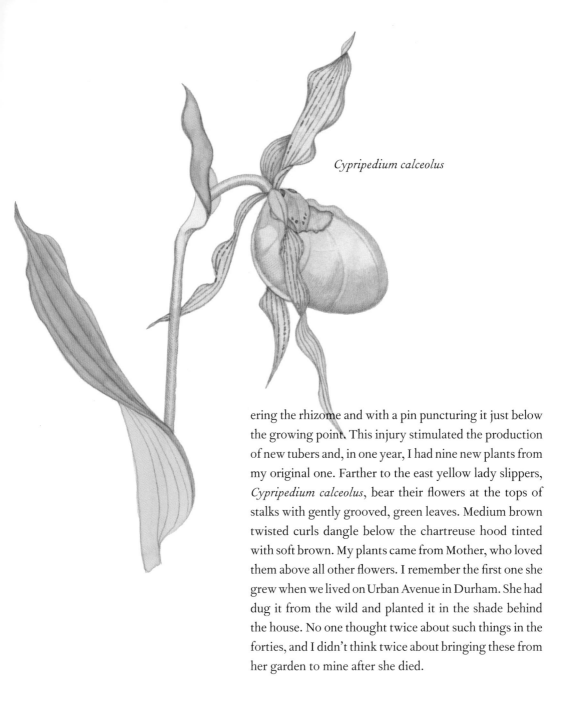

Cypripedium calceolus

ering the rhizome and with a pin puncturing it just below the growing point. This injury stimulated the production of new tubers and, in one year, I had nine new plants from my original one. Farther to the east yellow lady slippers, *Cypripedium calceolus*, bear their flowers at the tops of stalks with gently grooved, green leaves. Medium brown twisted curls dangle below the chartreuse hood tinted with soft brown. My plants came from Mother, who loved them above all other flowers. I remember the first one she grew when we lived on Urban Avenue in Durham. She had dug it from the wild and planted it in the shade behind the house. No one thought twice about such things in the forties, and I didn't think twice about bringing these from her garden to mine after she died.

MAY

Tony and Frances Bradshaw came from London in early May to celebrate the publication of his new book, *A Bloomsbury Canvas*. We invited friends with an interest in the Bloomsbury Group, and he invited those met through his art gallery, The Bloomsbury Workshop. Guests will come from all along the East Coast so we anxiously watched every weather forecast. This will be the largest party we have ever had and the house will be crowded if we must be inside. Each day the forecast for rain, given with greater certainty, was received with greater gloom. Finally, on Thursday we ordered a tent to protect our guests, the food, and drinks.

When the day came the weather was glorious for the garden but dreadful for our party. We had continuous rain and were consoled only because it was steady and gentle, without wind or thunder. Ippy set up an exhibit of drawings in the building where she works, near the woodsplitter. Ippy's building, ca. 1830, was formerly an old kitchen decaying behind a house in Hillsborough. Craufurd purchased it and Wayne Hall reconstructed it board by board on its current site in about 1990.

I arranged flowers from the garden for the house Saturday morning. We opened the blinds and shutters to let in natural light and, finally, turned on all the lights. Because we live in considerable darkness in order to protect the collection, we were happy to see the pictures, ceramics, and fabrics more clearly. Shortly before five o'clock Tony and Frances took their places in the living room. Craufurd became bartender for the afternoon, and I assumed responsibility for damage control and disaster prevention. The temperature hovered around fifty-three degrees.

The first visitors walked up the drive dressed more appropriately for winter than late spring, and from then on the party had its own momentum. I wore a raincoat and waterproof garden shoes the entire time as I came into

and out of the house. People who went through the garden kindly commented that it was appropriate to have British weather for such an occasion, but I was disappointed. Daisy Thorp, a friend and gardener in Chapel Hill, wrote in a note to us, "It [the garden] glimmered through the gray, misty veil. It was a ghost garden—haunting and lovely." The next morning the clouds vanished and cool, clear air replaced the damp cold that marred the party. We missed it by a day!

The season has changed and I am losing the battered, uneasy feeling that accompanies spring. Surely we won't have frost after the second week of May. Plants came out of the greenhouses and basement. We took cuttings of solenostemons (coleus) and salvias for the summer and fall garden and potted up young, recently rooted tender grasses we hope will be massive by summer's end. I feel a surge of excitement as we plan our color combinations. We will use chartreuse, red, and deepest burgundy behind the law office. The May Garden will have pink, purple, red, blue, and white flowers. I will plant the pale agastaches and salvias in the Soft Color Garden and the brightest flowers — orange, red, and yellow dahlias — in the neighboring Bright Color Garden.

May is the month for roses. Their show begins with the enormous chestnut rose, *Rosa roxburghii* f. *normalis*, first noted for its peeling bark in winter, now with delicate, single pink flowers open above a prickly calyx. That same calyx will expand to cover heps, or seedpods, that resemble painful to handle covers on chestnuts. Our plant is about nine feet tall after fifteen years while its double-flowered neighbor, *R. roxburghii* f. *roxburghii*, is less vigorous. In the May Garden *Rosa* 'Speedy Gonzales', a climbing sport of *R*. 'Martha Gonzales', blooms with blood-red flowers and near-white centers and brightens the burgundy-leaved barberry, *Berberis* x *ottawensis* 'Superba', through which it twists and turns.

Temperature shifts from summer to spring and back to summer bring roses to their peak in mid-May, about a week earlier than usual. *R*. 'Mary Wallace' covers the main arbor leading to the Tropical Garden with masses of semi-double pink flowers. Rugosas, with roughly sculptured, dark green leaves, brighten almost every bed. We smell the single pink flowers on *R*. 'Fru Dagmar Hastrup' as we walk up the hill from the cold frames and the intense mauve-pink flowers of *R*. 'Scabrosa' on the east side of the Tropical Garden. A combination of rose scents greets us as we approach the lath house. *R*. 'The Garland' intermingles with other roses, honeysuckles, and clematis nearby and hangs from the rafters on the west side.

I like best the roses that remind me of friends and

Rosa roxburghii f. *normalis*

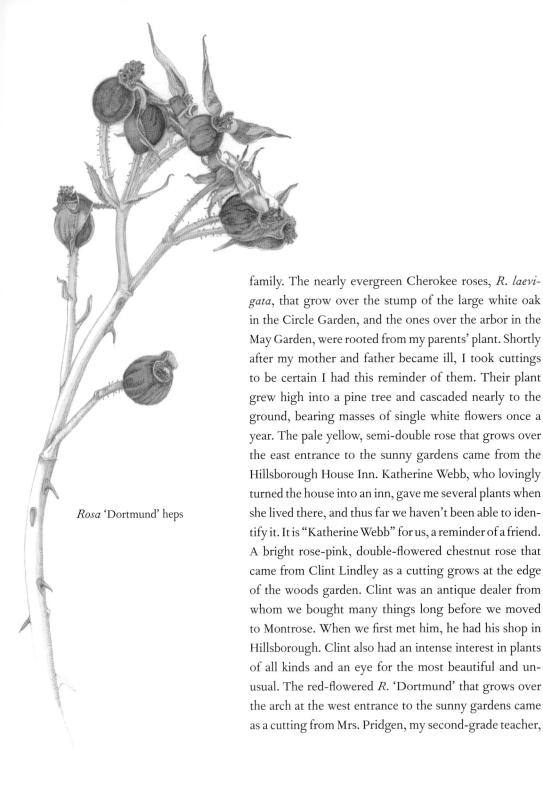

Rosa 'Dortmund' heps

family. The nearly evergreen Cherokee roses, *R. laevigata*, that grow over the stump of the large white oak in the Circle Garden, and the ones over the arbor in the May Garden, were rooted from my parents' plant. Shortly after my mother and father became ill, I took cuttings to be certain I had this reminder of them. Their plant grew high into a pine tree and cascaded nearly to the ground, bearing masses of single white flowers once a year. The pale yellow, semi-double rose that grows over the east entrance to the sunny gardens came from the Hillsborough House Inn. Katherine Webb, who lovingly turned the house into an inn, gave me several plants when she lived there, and thus far we haven't been able to identify it. It is "Katherine Webb" for us, a reminder of a friend. A bright rose-pink, double-flowered chestnut rose that came from Clint Lindley as a cutting grows at the edge of the woods garden. Clint was an antique dealer from whom we bought many things long before we moved to Montrose. When we first met him, he had his shop in Hillsborough. Clint also had an intense interest in plants of all kinds and an eye for the most beautiful and unusual. The red-flowered *R.* 'Dortmund' that grows over the arch at the west entrance to the sunny gardens came as a cutting from Mrs. Pridgen, my second-grade teacher, who, we later learned, was the model for Miss Dove in *Good Morning Miss Dove*, a novel by Frances Gray Patton. When I was in the fourth grade, we lived on the same street as Mrs. Pridgen and I was terrified of her. Shortly after we moved to Hillsborough we visited her in Durham, where I was astonished and relieved to discover that she was quite a small person with a sense of humor. Her rose blooms continuously all summer, slowly releases its dark green, shining leaves in late fall, and retains its bright red heps well into winter.

We have no rose garden, as such, even though there was one near the vegetable garden when we moved here. We saved those roses and incorporated them into all the other beds. Only *R.* 'Aloha' grows where we found it in the sunny gardens. The sweetheart rose, *R.* 'Cécile Brünner', one of my mother's favorites, now lives between the shrub border and the Aster Border. We added many china roses, because I like their red flowers and healthy, burgundy-tinted foliage, and rugosas for their vigor, hardiness, and textured leaves. And we added other roses selected for healthy foliage and fragrance. We never spray any of them and feed them with Rose-Tone twice a year—in early spring and just after their first flush of bloom in May.

The heat early in the month ended the iris display so important in the Blue and Yellow Garden. As they resume their yearly role as foliage plants, larkspur replaces them with spikes of rabbit-eared flowers, mostly in shades of blue. Their companion plant, love-in-a-mist, *Nigella damascena*, blooms with blue flowers surrounded by a ruff of thread-like leaves. After the flower is pollinated, the

Nigella damascena

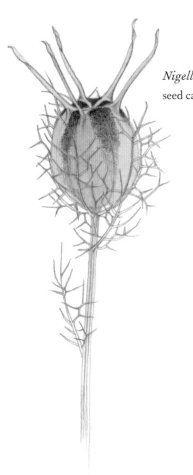

Nigella damascena
seed capsule

petals fall away, leaving a globular puff which swells as it ripens into a beige capsule filled with seeds.

Slender, candle-like panicles of buds cover the bottle-brush buckeye, *Aesculus parviflora*, at the entrance to the woods garden. I first saw this magnificent shrub in Durham when I had arrived with my mother's birthday cake long before the appointed hour and stopped by the Duke Gardens. I wandered into the Blomquist Garden of native plants and along one path saw a mound of green above which white, fluffy candles seemed to float like a splendid birthday cake. Now I have a similar display to remind me of that day. Ed Steffek was the curator of the garden at that time and when I confessed to searching for an old seed that might have been lying somewhere nearby, he told me he always harvested all of them. Both Ed and my mother are dead now, but recurring events of this season bring them back.

Aesculus parviflora in bud

Aesculus parviflora flowers

The sounds in the garden shift from spring to summer. Brilliant trills and flashes of iridescent blue feathers from indigo buntings accompany us in the sunny gardens and at the edge of the woods. We already miss the quavering songs of white-throated sparrows. A pair of wrens built a nest again in the big greenhouse. I wish they chose better places. One year they built in a large pot of echeverias and they almost always have at least one "litter" in the garage. In 1999 they built on top of a new pair of gloves placed on a shelf in the potting room in mid-morning. I found the finished nest the next day. That young family had a short life, even though we kept the doors closed and the windows open to prevent cats from discovering the nest. A snake got in before the young were old enough to fly, tore up the nest, and ate the young birds. The wrens tried again to build in the same place that year, but I removed the nest before it was finished.

Arisaema triphyllum in the Metasequoia Garden has small flowers and leaves like a typical jack-in-the-pulpit. Some plants have green flowers with lighter green stripes while others, the "Zebrinum" form, have dark chocolate stripes that extend into the interior of the spathe. The stench of another aroid greeted me in the greenhouse one afternoon. I knew I had removed all the sauromatums and amorphophalluses but further inspection revealed the first flower on a biarum grown from seed many years ago. The name on the label is *Narcissus viridiflorus*, a species I have long sought and never found, but it ain't no narcissus.

Arisaema triphyllum 'Zebrinum' form

It is just *Biarum* species here. I like these smelly plants with their fascinating flowers in spite of their scent. Other foul-smelling aroids bloom near the driveway. Handsome *Arum dioscoridis* fills the air with the smell of rotting meat. Its dark purple, spotted spathe bends away from the purple-black spadix to reveal a white and green throat. *A. palaestinum*, blooming now in the woods, is similar except that its cloak is dark red-violet.

Bletilla formosana x *striata*, a hardy terrestrial orchid, bloomed profusely this spring. The leaf tips of most bletillas in the open sections of the Circle Garden were browned by late frosts, but this hybrid below the wall near the big greenhouse was undamaged. Many outward-facing flowers of medium mauve-pink open day after day on stalks rising above linear, pleated leaves. We propagate bletillas as we do the calanthes in the woods by

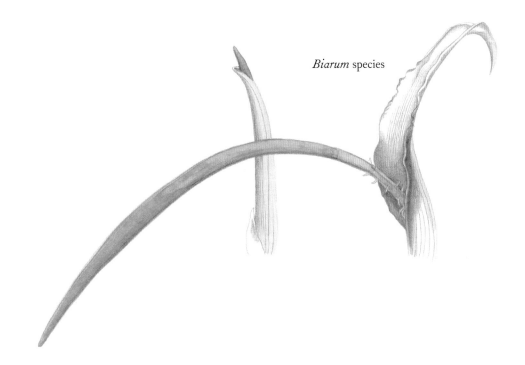

Biarum species

twisting off and replanting the back bulbs that otherwise would eventually disintegrate. The resulting new plants usually bloom the next spring. *Acanthus spinosus*, its hybrid *A*. 'Summer Beauty', and *A. hungaricus* bloom in shade or sun on stalks two or three feet high. Stiff spiny bracts all along the stalk separate pairs of flowers, each at a right angle to the set above it, and hoods of medium purple cover the papery white petals.

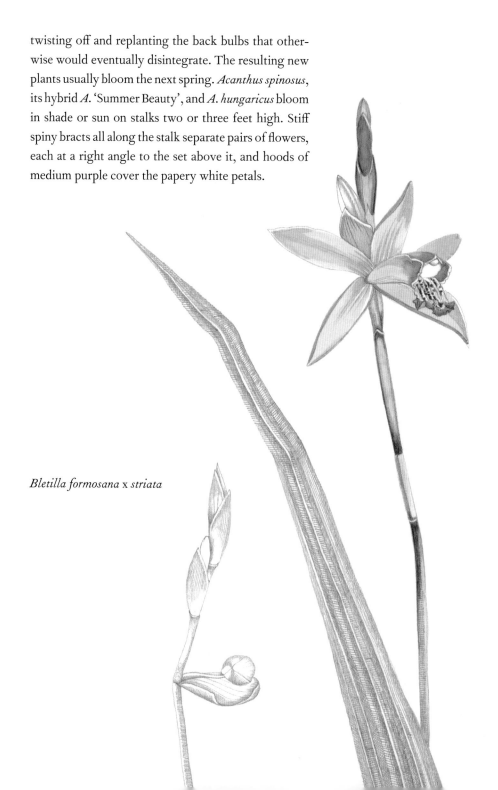

Bletilla formosana x *striata*

Acanthus spinosus

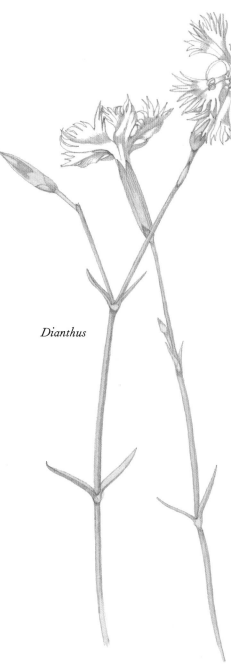

Dianthus

The Dianthus Walk continues to improve. Many phloxes bloomed and the freshly rooted dianthuses formed silvery gray or green mounds. Only a few fringed, fragrant, white flowers greet me on my early morning walks but there is hope that next year my days will begin again with a walk through a clove-scented garden. All gardeners must believe in next year.

Brienne (Brie) Gluvna joined the staff in the middle of the month. She was a student at Purdue when she worked here as an intern two years ago. I nearly rejected her application, for she stated she was looking for greenhouse experience and we have very little greenhouse work. She assured me she would do anything so I gave her a chance. I remember her first visit to Montrose. She drove around to the parking area in a car that sounded as if it were about to collapse and she brought her dog, Cally, with her. "A dog!" I exclaimed. "We have cats here." When she left in August she promised to come back. Brie is thin, about five feet three inches tall, with long, medium brown hair streaked with gold in summer and usually pulled back and fastened with a rubber band. She is well organized and focuses on each task until she completes it. Now Cally comes to work with her, and although the cats keep their distance, I believe they will be friends before the month is over.

It seems enough to have to worry about the lack of rain, weeds and how to get rid of them, and how to manage the wide variety of plants that grow in the gardens. Now we also worry about young wrens recently hatched in the big greenhouse. When I look into the nest all I see are wide-open mouths. The parents hover inside and outside the greenhouse. One sits in the *Prunus mume* near the building and screams the alarm as I approach. We have two major problems. One, I usually have a cat or two running ahead or behind me. Two, early last week I found a large snakeskin near the cooler on the west side of the greenhouse, and on Friday saw an enormous black-snake inside the greenhouse. I don't know how to protect them. If I close the doors, the parent birds won't be able to get in to feed their young or keep them warm. I opened the doors during the day, closed them at night, and miraculously these little birds survived and flew out of the greenhouse to live in the garden.

Roger spent a day in the potting room. We couldn't understand his inter-est until we discovered he had cornered a skink and bitten off its brilliant blue tail. We were accustomed to meeting this little lizard almost every time we entered the building, so we protected him with barricades to keep the cat away from him. The skink's head turned red and he could barely walk. We banished Roger to the house. I believe we saved the skink for we have seen a tailless lizard several times since.

In search of the most beautiful or interesting clematises for Ippy to draw, we found *Clematis* 'Gravetye Beauty' in a heap on the ground. Then we saw, six feet up on the arbor, a young woodchuck standing on one branch with his forearms draped over a higher one. He appeared to be sleeping. Although he slowly acknowledged our presence by moving his head, he made no attempt to clatter his teeth or run away. An hour later we found him in the same position.

We have had a desert environment this spring with thin air, clear blue skies, low humidity, and warm days. We complain only because the soil is dry. Although the garden looks lush, the grass is skimpy and the ground is hard. It turned cold late in the month with temperatures in the upper thirties and low forties for two successive nights. I was happy because cool temperatures prolonged the rose display, but worried because most tender plants are out of the greenhouses now and solenostemons hate anything below fifty degrees. We survived without major damage. Solenostemons from the warm basement adjusted to the outside temperatures with only a touch of frost burn. We were lucky for they are vulnerable to everything — sunburn, frost, and over- or under-watering.

Most plants emerged from the greenhouses ready to grow. The small greenhouse attached to the house is primarily a home for bulbs and is also where we keep flats of cyclamen, freshly germinated seeds, and tender garden plants such as *Breynia nivosa* 'Rosea Picta' (snowbush), *Pennisetum setaceum* (fountain grass), and *Euphorbia cotinifolia*. On the window shelves, pots of young narcissus seedlings and their seed parents grow all winter. Back-up pots of all the rain lilies assure me I will have a supply even after the worst imaginable winter. Because summer is the greatest challenge for bulbs in pots, we must decide which to dry off completely, which to keep barely moist, and which to maintain in regularly moist soil. When we reach our conclusion, we write it on a label inserted into the pot.

The larger greenhouse, a detached building near the parking lot, was built in the late 1980s. It is the winter home for salvias, most plectranthus species and forms, abutilons, cannas, phormiums, and other nearly hardy plants, plus several heating mats for propagation. These plants, plus agaves, echeverias, and lantanas, must withstand temperatures just above freezing at about thirty-eight degrees. Solenostemons, a few plectranthuses, and *Hibiscus acetosella* spend their winters in the warmer basement. Acclimatizing plants after their winter coddling is tricky. We take them first into a shaded area, then into part sun, and finally into full sun before we plant them in the garden. It takes two to three weeks to prepare them for their summer homes and I learned the hard way that I can't rush Mother Nature. The hard way is often the best.

We worked on the Color Gardens, looking critically at all four beds that surround the big urn. Sometimes it is difficult, but necessary, to sacrifice plants growing well in the wrong place. This week I removed masses of *Salvia guaranitica*, replanting a few clumps in the center of the two western quadrants and putting the remainder on the brush pile. We eliminated most castor beans, leaving only two or three in the southern sections. We dug and discarded blue irises from the northeast Black, White, and Red Garden. Brightly colored dahlias went into the hot color quadrant, red verbenas into the red bed, and pastel salvias into the Soft Color Garden. A common thread of dark burgundy foliage of *Berberis thunbergii* f. *atropurpurea* unifies all four gardens.

We are intensely critical of this garden and think constantly in terms of color, form, and texture. Problems arise because I often think in terms of living plants and how long it took me to grow them in such numbers or so well. It takes a disciplined, tough-minded gardener to create an aesthetically exciting garden. It is difficult for me; I care most about the plants.

It was a mistake to relax and think the frosts were over. We had record low temperatures toward the end of May with frost one morning and more record low temperatures the next week, followed by record high ones. Because of ninety-degree heat by mid-afternoon, I wore a hat and lathered on sunscreen, but I worked outside all day, staying in the shade at least part of the time and drinking gallons of water.

During the 1930s the Grahams built a garage southeast of the house. This unpretentious structure protects two cars, the recycling containers, and an old bookshelf for equipment. Old license plates reflecting the career of Sandy Graham, our immediate predecessor, line the top of the walls. Most of the license plate numbers are low, culminating in one with the number two when he was lieutenant governor of North Carolina. A small room south of the parking section of the building holds tools, garden furniture, and a compressor to pump up the tires on garden carts and lawn mowers.

A bell, formerly used for calling in the farm hands for lunch, rests tilted on the roof ready to ring again and a weathervane signals weather changes better than any forecasters. The building is made of load-bearing tiles, originally designed as dividers for interior rooms in large office buildings. They retain their natural colors: copper red and purple red, a difficult background for a garden. The same tiles, painted white, were added to the exterior of the old kitchen.

Dark purple and pale yellow are the best colors for this background of unpainted tiles. *Rosa* 'Mermaid', espaliered against the wall, produces large, pale yellow flowers with a crown of golden stamens all summer. Root suckers, perfect miniatures of the larger plant, appear a little way out from the original plant each summer. We call them "Mermaidettes" and dig and pot them for sale or move them to other parts of the garden. *Trachelospermum asiaticum* clings to the tile behind the rose where it has clusters of fragrant, creamy white flowers in late spring. White-flowered *Clematis patens* intertwines with the rose and blooms in mid-May while the intense purple *C.* 'Jackmanii' waits until later. In summer the dark purple, small-waisted bells of *C. pitcheri* hang from clasping stems.

Rosa 'Mermaid'

Clematis patens

Chartreuse leaves of *Ligustrum* 'Vicaryi' brighten the bed in summer and purple ones match the tiles in winter. Clusters of dark purple flowers of *Campanula glomerata* 'Joan Elliott' open in May while *Phlomis russeliana*, its neighbor, covers the south end of this garden with large, felted, medium-green heart-shaped leaves and stems bearing whorls of pale yellow, paw-like flowers. Rabbits and deer haven't yet found the creamy yellow and green succulent leaves of *Sedum erythrostictum* 'Mediovariegatum', formerly *S. alboroseum*. Fragrant, star-flowered *Jasminum officinale* clambers through wire supports attached to the wall behind a seedling barberry, *Berberis thunbergii* f. *atropurpurea*, with leaves that match the tiles on the garage. This white-flowered, hardy jasmine was on the property when we arrived and, though we left it where we found it near the pump house, we moved rooted pieces to other gardens. *Arundo donax* var. *versicolor*, the giant reed, dominates the southern corner of the garage bed with bright white young foliage vertically striped with green. As the stalk grows to its fall height of twelve feet

Arundo donax var. *versicolor*

or more, the colors will soften—white turns cream and dark green turns medium green. Mere hints of its variegation remain in fall.

Racemes of medium purple flowers on *Salvia jurisicii* that bloomed earlier this spring are replaced now by red-violet spikes on *Teucrium hircanicum*. Several plants of neighboring *Ballota acetabulosa* have clusters of pale green miniature saucers in the axils of their soft gray-green leaves. Large clumps of *Yucca flaccida* with tall stalks draped with creamy white flowers dominate the northern edge of the bed. These architectural plants are attractive at every stage—buds in shades of purple and green open to white flowers tinged with light green or pink. Dark purple-leaved *Sedum* 'Purple Emperor' grows at the yuccas' base and *Hedera helix* 'Goldheart' (now *H. h.* 'Oro di Bogliasco', but I'm not sure I will use its proper name) and the climbing hydrangea, *H. anomala* subsp. *petiolaris*, cover the north end of the garage. The hydrangea won't cling to the tiles so the ivy that grows over and around it holds it against the wall.

Late May is an in-between time in the garden. The spring wildflowers have finished and most summer ones haven't begun. We cut away the old bloom stalks of euphorbias, hellebores, phloxes, and irises in the Rock and Metasequoia Gardens. We cut *Chrysogonum virginianum* all the way to the ground—flower stalks, leaves, everything. Although they are still blooming, mildewed leaves and leggy growth mar their beauty. This severe pruning stimulates fresh growth with no sign of blight and flowers from now until winter.

We began to plant our pots and urns by the end of the month. As I began to develop the land at Montrose, I resolved to make a garden not dependent on irrigation. I searched for plants that would grow well in our climate, which often includes long dry periods in summer. Plantings in pots and urns enable us to grow plants that cannot survive my miserly watering policy. Craufurd found most of our assortment of Victorian urns, usually set on pedestals or atop posts in the stone wall. He also bought cast iron cooking vessels for us to use as planters. Our largest one, in the Scree Garden, was used originally to extract salt from seawater. The other really large ones were used to make sorghum molasses, to scald a pig, or to make large quantities of stew. The smaller pots were for washing clothes or cooking jams and other foods. We paint some and leave those with attractive patinas unpainted. Most have drainage holes but some remain intact for bog-loving plants such as colocasias and papyrus. These containers are durable, requiring little or no maintenance, and most remain outside, unprotected all winter.

The "bathtub," a large, oval, cast iron urn at the end of the Aster Border, is an important feature in the late-summer gardens. We anticipate the peak season by filling it with foliage and flowering plants that perform all summer: dark purple-flowered, fragrant petunias, cerise-flowered calabrachoas, verbenas with purple or pink flowers, and white *Lantana montevidensis*. Long graceful branches of *Coprosma* x *kirkii* 'Kirkii Variegata' hang over the edges of the urn and, with the silver-leaved *Senecio viravira*, will be visible in the evening light. Bright cerise *Iresine herbstii* will be brilliant when fall's slanting light shines through it.

The "big urn," our largest cast iron container, is on a brick pedestal in the center of the paths separating the beds that make up the Color Gardens. Standing on a ladder, we set in plants from all four surrounding areas. In the center we placed vertical, dark burgundy *Pennisetum setaceum* 'Rubrum' that will eventually form a towering fountain of leaves. We added *Canna* 'Tropicana' with foliage that combines the chartreuse, red, green, and burgundy of all the gardens in each leaf. Chartreuse-leaved sweet potatoes went along the edges to hang over the urn on all sides. Bright red verbenas and a black and green solenostemon like those in the Black, Red, and White Garden will eventually dangle over the side.

A small terra-cotta pot at the corner of the brightest Color Garden is

Acalypha wilkesiana

planted with solenostemons, *Acalypha wilkesiana* (copperleaf), *Verbena* 'Batesville Rose', and a lead-gray phormium grown from seed many years ago. The planting is both somber and brilliant.

The Albert Memorial, a tall, elaborate urn, is vaguely reminiscent of its namesake in Hyde Park in London. It stands at the western end of the walk that begins at the eastern edge of the sunny gardens. This path between Jo's Bed and the Blue and Yellow Garden provides a view through the curved arches of the lath house and through the shrub border to the fence and this urn. A row of junipers near the edge of our property at the bottom of the field between us and Cameron Park Elementary School provides the background for the urn. We need bright colors to show up against their dark, somber foliage, so we planted the upright shell ginger (*Alpinia zerumbet* 'Variegata'), chartreuse-leaved sweet potatoes (*Ipomoea batatas* 'Margarita'), a brilliant chartreuse jasmine (*Jasminum officinale* 'Aureum'), and potato vine (*Solanum laxum* 'Aureovariegatum'). Dark, burgundy-leaved solenostemons provide the necessary contrast.

The most important urn in front of the house, in the center of the front walk to the Circle Garden, was placed there for traffic control. Shortly after we planted that garden, a large group of visitors came for a tour, after which we discovered tire tracks through the center of the garden. Half the tracks were on the gravel and the other half three feet into the bed. One dreadful visitor drove into the center circle and turned east to exit, crushing plants and hopes for our freshly planted garden. This urn, the automobile deterrent, is so large no vehicle can hit it without damage to itself. A large, dark-leaved phormium is surrounded by trailing silver-leaved plants that show up in dim light, and a burgundy solenostemon, *S.* 'Religious Radish', warms the colors.

We planted the pair of large urns near the front door as they have been for years. Upright dark burgundy *Alternanthera dentata* 'Rubiginosa' surrounds a silver-leaved *Plectranthus argentatus* in the center. The variegated *Plectranthus madagascariensis* 'Variegated Mintleaf', *Coprosma* x *kirkii* 'Kirkii Variegata', *Petunia integrifolia*, *Tradescantia pallida* 'Purpurea', and a white-flowered form of *Lantana montevidensis* will eventually grow over the edge.

Plants that require constantly moist conditions grow in "bog pots," containers without drainage holes. A large, dark-leaved elephant's ear, *Colocasia esculenta* 'Black Magic', went into the large copper vessel in the Blue and Yellow Garden. To brighten the planting we added *Acorus gramineus* 'Ogon' (grassy-leaved sweet flag), *Rhynchospora colorata* (formerly *Dichromena colorata*, white-topped sedge), and *Lysimachia nummularia* 'Aurea' (yellow creeping jenny). Finally we added papyrus, *Cyperus papyrus*, a gift from Ron Franklin, a friend who helped Wayne Hall build the lath house and restore and maintain the other buildings on the property. The second bog pot, at the west side of the lath house, contains *Rhynchospora colorata*, *Petasites japonicus* (sweet coltsfoot), and *Iris ensata*.

It takes time for the gardens in urns to flow together. The plants that drape over the rims must grow long enough to hang down below the edges. The upright plants must grow tall enough to rise above the others. They look a little forced and uncomfortable just after we plant them in early summer. I would worry more if I hadn't created such plantings for nearly twenty years.

Other creatures that live on this land often interrupt our activities. I met a turtle that, on first noticing me, pulled herself into her shell. When I looked into the shell, she opened her mouth, but not to hiss. I opened mine in a similar manner. She did it again, and I imitated her. Then she extended her bright yellow legs and let me rub the pads of her feet. She seemed to enjoy it and so did I.

In mid-afternoon one day we heard a great commotion near the bluebird box on the Yucca Bank. A pair of bluebirds hopped and flew about, clearly agitated. We saw about four inches of snake protruding from the entrance to the box, so got a ladder and climbed high enough to open the lid and see the rest of a large blacksnake in the soft, moss-lined nest. We inserted a stick into his coiled body and threw him out of the nest, hoping not to hurt him but to save the young birds. We were too late; the nest contained no birds.

We also found a nest inside the copper pitcher that hangs on a post near the little fountain in the lath house. Carolina wrens had built a messy nest with sticks coming out of the top of the pot, and a narrow bowl at the base where eggs and parents were hidden. This unfortunate choice of a home will fill with water if we have a heavy rain. No rain is in sight, so perhaps this little family will survive long enough to fly away.

Cathy spends hours each day taking cuttings of tender plants necessary for our grand finale in the fall. We need masses of salvias, solenostemons, plectranthus, and other heat-loving tender perennials to create the abundance of foliage and flowers so important to the sunny beds. Cathy has a remarkable talent for propagation and seldom fails to produce the desired plants. Successful propagation requires sensitivity to each plant's needs and habits. She seems to know when and where to take the cuttings, which strength of rooting hormone to use, and when to pot on the rooted plants.

By the end of May the garden near Ippy's building, the new old kitchen, is in full bloom with late-spring annuals. The billowing leaves of the sumptuous purple mustard, *Brassica juncea* 'Red Giant', have broad, light green, basal veins and dark purple or red-violet lobes. The succulent, chartreuse leaves of neighboring *Talinum calycinum* seem almost satiny when compared to the rough-textured mustard. There are both single- and double-flowered bright orange calendulas. But the brilliant yellow or orange California poppies, *Eschscholzia californica*, are the stars. Their blue-green leaves are like the finest filaments of tarnished copper and their flowers glow with great intensity. I like best the bright yellow flowers with centers gently tinged with orange. Red and scarlet rhoeas poppies, *Papaver rhoeas*, bloom throughout the bed with paper-like flowers. Most have four petals arranged as two pairs set at right angles to each other. Young flowers have a horizontal lower set of petals and a vertical upper set and look like cups resting in saucers. Most of our poppies have black basal blotches and an explosion of stamens, green when young and purple at maturity. Honeybees quiver in the centers of the flowers, making them

Eschscholzia californica

Papaver rhoeas

Berberis thunbergii f. atropurpurea

tremble even on windless days. Dark burgundy-flowered bachelor buttons, *Centaurea cyanus*, nearly match the mustard's leaves. A ring of boxwoods, *Buxus sempervirens* 'Suffruticosa', borders a circle mulched with gravel and lined with cast iron chairs. Few people sit here, partly because these chairs are always hard and hot when the sun is on them.

I realized during the night that the planting in the big urn was wrong. The canna has all the right colors but the wrong form. It is too rigid, so out it came and we replaced it with *Solenostemon* 'Bellingrath'. We may change it again before summer ends. That urn is the main focal point when viewing the sunny gardens through the main entrance to the Tropical Garden. It is the centerpiece when we enter the Blue and Yellow Garden from the east and look through all the gardens to the field beyond, and it must tie all of these gardens together. Chartreuse gives it life and links it to many of the gardens near the urn as well as beyond. Burgundy, the most important dark color in the gardens, relieves the fluff and provides a common thread through most of the borders. I need only to put up my hand and shut out burgundy plants to see how important they are.

Someone came to the door and inquired about a garden tour. I led her to the potting room where I gave her a brochure. She glanced at it and asked, "When will the garden be pretty? I want to see flowers." I took a deep breath and responded in my lowest, most controlled voice, "Late September." I am the wrong person to answer that ques-

Prunus persica (purple-leaved peach)

Cotinus coggygria 'Royal Purple'

tion. Each day has some plants at a peak, some ending their main show, and others just beginning to grow. I often find those just beginning to grow or bloom the most exciting and I think it is pretty every day. Besides, we always have flowers somewhere.

We celebrated Craufurd's birthday the last week in May. We surprised him with Cathy's super coconut cake and strong coffee at nine in the morning. And then we sang his version of "Happy Birthday":

Happy Birthday to you
Happy Birthday to you
Happy Birthday, dear Wally
Happy Birthday to you!

The first birthday party Craufurd attended as a child was for a little boy named Wally, and for years he thought those were the official words of the song. As he blew out the candles, I made my usual wish, that Charlemagne would come home. He was our beautiful ginger cat that disappeared when I was seven. All of my family always wishes for Charlemagne to reappear.

I ended the month spending a day out of the garden and ache to return to it.

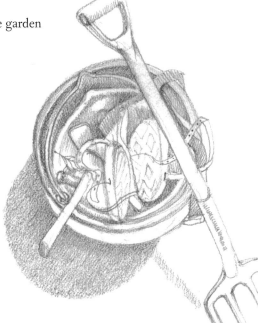

JUNE

The drought remains with us. A skimpy beige carpet of grass during dry periods in summer is normal but dry young leaves on saponarias and chrysogonums usually untouched by drought are not. Poppies that should be three or four feet high are less than a foot; each plant produces one flower instead of many.

I thinned the castor beans behind the law office, pulling out three-quarters of them and cutting off the tips of those that stay so they can withstand the strong winds of fall. We never stake them. I had nearly finished when Craufurd warned me of a severe thunderstorm warning for Orange County, so I pushed my cart under the law office, unplugged the computer, and turned off the air conditioning before the storm arrived. It was thrilling to stand at the front door and watch drifts of rain come down the front walk. Wind whipped branches around and rain washed away spring's pollen still coating their leaves. It was comforting to think it rained throughout the entire garden, in the woods, and even on the pond. When it was over, we guessed the amount we would find in the rain gauge and were both wrong. We had .58 of an inch—the most since mid-April. The garden responded. Now *Salvia sclarea* has fleshy, not limp, leaves and holds its clusters of blooms upright. The garden looks brighter and healthier, and I am optimistic about getting the growth we need this summer.

As usual I dug out the milk thistles too late. In winter *Silybum marianum* is a handsome, luxurious basal rosette of large green leaves overlaid with white splotches. It bloomed about two weeks ago with tufts of purple flowers, and goldfinches have nearly plucked them to pieces. The birds broke down the stalks and devoured the newly ripened seeds. Those birds eat and fly, dropping seeds and singing all the way. They usually travel in pairs going from the thistles to the nearest ripe poppy seedpod, where they sit

Papaver somniferum

on swaying stalks and shred the pods to get to the seeds. They let me come close enough to see them, but if I come too near, they fly away twittering as they go. It is always a race to see whether we can collect enough seeds for our needs before they completely devour the crop.

Now that most irises have finished blooming we cut their stalks at the top of each rhizome. *Iris foetidissima*, stinking gladwyn, in the northeast section of the Circle Garden, is an exception. This attractive, simple iris keeps its seedpods, for they hold a promise for late summer and

Iris foetidissima

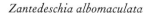

Zantedeschia albomaculata

fall beauty when they ripen and burst to reveal fleshy orange seeds. *Zantedeschia albomaculata*, calla lily, with large, arrow-shaped leaves splashed with white streaks and spots blooms on the east side of the Tropical Garden and throughout the May Garden where it has little water and full sun. The elegantly twisted, white flowers are among the most beautiful I know. The spathe begins green but turns whiter and whiter until, when fully opened, it is pure white with green only at the tip and base. Inside the curled flower a pale yellow spadix bears many white, thread-like filaments. As the seeds ripen the spathe turns green again and the seedhead eventually becomes so heavy it falls to the ground, depositing seeds fifteen inches or so away from the parent plant. I have picked only one flower in the many years I have grown this plant—the one Ippy drew.

Centaurea rothrockii, a large bachelor's button in the Circle Garden, has thistle-like heads made up of masses of thread-like, white, sterile flowers below a puff of smaller fertile ones on stalks at least three feet high. Last year all but one plant had pink flowers and so far this year all are white. Beige buds with geometric patterns of brown triangles overlaid with fine, hair-like netting are as beautiful as the flowers.

We collect every possible drop of water from the infrequent showers that delight us when they come, and frustrate us when they end so quickly. Over the years Craufurd has bought many large copper or brass cooking pots from antique shops near here and placed them at the drip line of the eaves of the barn, smokehouse, and law office. A good shower can fill them with enough water for all of the planted pots and urns. Thus far this year the containers have never been full.

Centaurea rothrockii

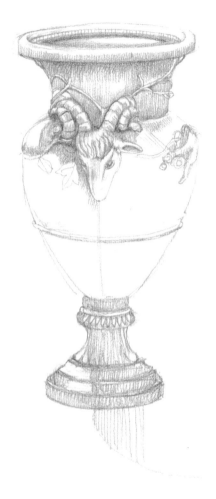

At an auction recently, Craufurd bought a pair of large, cast iron urns embossed with mythological characters and decorated with goat heads as handles. We placed these, the Capricorn Urns, at the top of the stairs leading to the Blue and Yellow Garden and now must decide whether and how to paint and plant them.

I finished my work in the sun around four thirty one afternoon and Roger and I went to the woods, where it was cooler. He is more sensitive to heat than I and pants audibly. He stayed with me while I weeded the Mother-in-Law Walk, pulling out microstegium and other grasses and young tree seedlings. The soil, though dry, remains friable enough to pull out most weeds by their roots without digging, so I made rapid progress. When the time came to go in, I couldn't find the little gray cat. After a long search, I saw him hunched up, then pouncing, on a blacksnake about five feet long. He doesn't know to fear snakes yet. The snake hissed and struck out at him, but Roger was undeterred and drove him under a *Cephalotaxus harringtonii* (plum yew) where, because of dense foliage, I could see neither of them. After futile pleading for thirty minutes, I poked a stick gently into the branches, drove the cat out, grabbed him, and took him to the house. Cat and snake survived and perhaps both learned something!

In early June we celebrated our forty-fourth wedding anniversary. When I said the first forty-four are the hardest, meaning that every year is even better than the last, I was dismayed to hear someone defend Craufurd, saying he seems a very pleasant person, who must be nice enough to live with. We celebrated by dining at an excellent restaurant in Durham. I dressed up as much as is possible for one who lives only in work clothes and wore a lovely old pendant he gave me on another anniversary. We talked about the future of this place and of what we must do to make it secure. It was a delightful, quiet evening. I thought back to previous anniversary dinners. At first we had no idea of what our life would hold or where we would live. We wanted to travel before we settled down, so we planned imaginary trips. After several years, we talked about what kind of house we would like. By then Craufurd knew he would continue to teach and write. I thought I would teach piano and harpsichord, play duets and trios with friends, keep house, and entertain our friends.

After we bought a house in Durham, I planted a garden, filling our acre of land within two years. I read every book and many articles by Elizabeth Lawrence, quickly became obsessed with plants, and wanted to grow everything desirable and possible in central North Carolina. After that, we spoke of plants and gardens at our anniversary dinners. When I ran out of land, our anniversary talks returned to discussions about the kind of house we wanted and the amount of land needed to satisfy my curiosity about plants and combinations. It was no longer satisfying just to grow a plant well; I wanted to make an aesthetically pleasing garden. We took pad and pencil to restaurants during those years and drew sketches of houses with gardens inside and out. Fortunately, we didn't have to build our dream house. We found Montrose and six years later I started Montrose Nursery. After that our anniversary discussions centered on goals and problems of running a nursery. The problems overwhelmed the goals and I had little time for the garden, so I closed the nursery, and finally, after thirty-six years of marriage, began to realize my dream. Now we speak of our remaining time here and the uses for Montrose after we die. This year we believe we are on the verge of finding the best solution possible for the future of this land and its garden.

When we returned home and I discovered I had lost my pendant, it destroyed the occasion. I relived every moment of the evening and called the restaurant. I described us, what we wore, where we sat, gave the name of our waitress, and waited, only to be told they couldn't find it. I couldn't sleep thinking of where else I could have dropped my precious pendant. We got up at five in the morning and drove back to the restaurant to hunt for it unsuccessfully in the parking lot. After we returned home, I walked back and forth across the lawn between the garage and the house examining every clump of browned grass. I did this about a dozen times. We went about our routine chores on Saturday morning, but the thought of my carelessness haunted me. In the afternoon I worked in the woods, always a place of renewal for me. Just before dinner, I looked again in the car, and found my beautiful old pendant on the floor behind my seat. I will never wear it again.

Craufurd and I brought the last three pots out from the greenhouse. This is always a challenge. Because these are our heaviest containers, we need a dolly to take them from house to garden. We carried large pots of *Phaius tankervilliae*, the nun's orchid, and *Clivia miniata* from the sunroom off the little greenhouse to the back terrace. Sometimes I wonder, why bother? Then I remember. The orchid was a gift from a friend, is now enormous, I can grow it well, and it has bloomed faithfully for fifteen or more years. The clivia came from our garden in Durham twenty-five years ago. It didn't flower for about ten years until I realized clivias need to be pot-bound, so now I move it outside, in its pot, for the summer when I water it daily and fertilize it every two weeks. It comes inside again shortly before frost and receives no water until flower buds appear in February.

The third plant was the greatest challenge. *Agave americana*, the century plant, spends the summer in the urn on the south side of the law office. Our magnificent but tender fifteen-year-old specimen must be protected inside during winter. The challenge comes when we transport it. Stiff, sharp spines along the leaf margins and at the end of each leaf seem designed to keep us at a distance. We wear protective goggles for our eyes, leather gloves for our arms and hands, and we carry the pot on its side, hoping the weight and angle won't break or bend any leaves. Agaves carry their history with them. If we crush or bend a leaf, the plant shows it as well as the imprint of next year's leaf. Transporting it is not a pleasant experience for either of us. "Lift it," he says. "I'm trying," I say. We always bend at least one leaf that must be removed. The heavy basal leaves I cut away this year were filled with moisture even though this agave received no water during winter. Every year we remove smaller offsets from the base of the plant and have young agaves ready to replace our old plant when it finally blooms and dies.

I worked nearly all day in the sun but was reprimanded and sent to the house for a thermos of ice water and a frozen collar, a terry cloth towel just a little larger than a face cloth. The frozen collar is the most cooling treatment I know. We thoroughly moisten towels, lay each one in a semi-circle in a plastic bag, put them into the freezer, and on really hot days take them, straight from the freezer, to drape around our necks. As they thaw, the water that drips onto our shirts cools us.

I weakened by mid-month and watered the scree. We created the Scree Garden in 1991 from a bit of lawn east of the big greenhouse. We covered the area with clear plastic in early summer and by July the intense heat beneath it had killed all the grass, weeds, and most seeds. I like to think the earthworms crept out as the temperature rose. We tilled in a large truckload of pea gravel to a depth of about twelve to eighteen inches, hoping for a balance of half soil and half gravel. Then we shaped this mixture into mounds to provide extra drainage for those plants that need it and valleys as paths for those who would tend or observe the plants. We added about four inches of gravel as mulch on top of the entire area, and began planting. This year Cathy brought carefully selected rocks covered with lichen or marked with streaks of gold, red, or gray from her farm in Person County to separate the scree from the surrounding lawn.

We planted this garden with cactuses, yuccas, and agaves that need good drainage and added small plants, including dianthus, veronicas, small geraniums, species narcissus, and miniature heucheras that might be smothered by the voluptuous growth of their neighbors in the main gardens. This, an experimental garden, is for survivors selected more for cultural needs than for form or color. Although some plants die here, many others will grow only in this environment.

The pump house, a small building southwest of the law office, covers and protects the well that used to provide all the water for the main house. A large storage tank that could hold five hundred gallons — enough water for the Graham family's needs — remains in the basement of the house. By the time we moved here, city water was available and the tank held furnace oil. The first time we ordered fuel, we asked the company to fill it. The provider said, "But Mr. Graham always ordered only three hundred gallons, and he ordered that after the tank was nearly empty." We couldn't imagine why, so went ahead with our original order only to discover a leak just above the three hundred gallon mark. Now we have a new oil tank.

The garden around the pump house has never been successful. I envisioned something so spectacular that visitors, driving around the front of the house, would want to walk the length of the lawn to see what was there. It has not happened. In early June we cut away large plants of sweet autumn clematis, *Clematis terniflora*; cut back Carolina jessamine, *Gelsemium sempervirens*; and tried to remove every scrap of chocolate vine, *Akebia trifoliata*. I first saw akebia in Italy when we spent a spring on Lake Como. Chocolate-colored flowers opened on a vine that grew through *Rosa* 'Mermaid' to the top of a twenty-foot wall and perfumed the terrace where we had wine

before lunch and dinner. I wanted to grow those plants to remind me of that happy spring and, after a considerable search, finally obtained both. The rose stays. Akebia has to go. It has grown up and through the pump house twisting itself over and around every plant that surrounds the building.

Smilax, *Smilax lanceolata*, on the north side, isn't the horrid weed that infests woods and hedges and causes even mild-mannered people to swear. By June thick, pliable, nearly thornless stalks have grown at least twelve feet long and begin to cover the barberries at its base. Tendrils curled at the tips like insect antennae dangle from the joints near the dark green, cupped appendages. I can place a stalk anywhere I want it to stay and the tendrils quickly

Smilax lanceolata

clasp their neighbors and secure the vine in place. In a few weeks shiny heart-shaped leaves will appear along with small, near-white flowers. This plant is handsome all winter and every summer I think I will cut it at Christmas for decoration on the mantle, but I have never decorated the mantle at Christmas so the plant remains in its entirety until late winter when I cut it to the ground. Shortly after moving here, I dug up its enormous white tuber thinking I was getting rid of it, but the bit I left sprouted, and now I appreciate its beauty.

Clint Lindley died on June 12. We received a call in mid-morning and drove to Yanceyville to be with Erich, his companion. Clint went as I would like to go. The previous day he worked in his garden, planting a new bed, and that evening he bought a wonderful old oriental rug at a bargain price. On the morning of his death, he went back to the garden, watered the plants again, and returned to the house to move furniture and place the new rug. Shortly thereafter Erich found him, dead from a heart attack. The problem with such deaths is timing. It was too soon for him to leave us. Clint was a gentle soul with a delightful sense of humor. We always had dinner together during Christmas week. I will think of him whenever I see his chestnut rose. We have something purchased from him in almost every room of our house. In my office in the law office, his early-nineteenth-century chest of drawers contains financial records, letters worth saving, and daily notes on the garden. In the adjacent room his cabinet filled with Bloomsbury pottery and porcelain is attached to the wall above his early coffer. We had similar taste and values.

In mid-June tender perennials went into the summer gardens despite temperatures in the nineties. We planted agastaches and *Justicia fulvicoma* in the Soft Color Garden and a brilliant crepe myrtle with dark foliage and orange-red flowers in the Bright Color Garden. *Salvia* 'Van-Houttei' went into the burgundy and silver section and we added salvias, grasses, and other perennials to the May Garden. The air was bad but there was a breeze; we wore frozen collars and drank copious amounts of water as we worked. We almost always plant with a garden fork, first digging as deeply as we can to bring up the clods of earth, and then, using a hand mattock, we break up the solid blocks of soil until they are tiny particles. We set in our plant, put a little Plantone nearby, and water deeply. Finally, we put a forkful of shredded leaves around the base of each plant to conserve the moisture we added and to keep the root zone cool. Many newly planted plants wilt in sun but revive in evening's shade. We water everything every other day until it rains. Blessed rain, what wouldn't I give for an inch a week!

Each week begins with a staff meeting, plans for each person for the week, and a discussion of problems and solutions. We share a sense of urgency at this season and can't stop planting just because the soil is dry. Many tours, a Garden Open Day, and a return visit from the selection committee of the Garden Conservancy are scheduled for fall and we have barely three months left to prepare the garden for its most spectacular season. We can't let it slip up on us.

By mid-June the large patch of *Mentha buddlejafolia* near the barn is at its peak. The name describes it perfectly. Silvery gray leaves all along fifteen-inch stalks look like those of buddlejas, and five or more spikes of mint-like, lavender flowers spread out from their tips. Unfortunately, it spreads like mint and now covers an area at least ten by fifteen feet. We pause each day to listen to the hum of thousands of insects, mostly wasps and bees, that hover over the plants and rest briefly on the flowers. This, the most beautiful music of the garden in early summer, reminds me of our visit in 1992 to Joe Eck and Wayne Winterrowd at their exquisite garden, North Hills, in southern Vermont. When the flowers fade, Craufurd will mow the entire area and fresh new stalks will appear within a month.

Only two plants of *Nigella papillosa* grew from the packet of seeds we planted near the wood splitter last winter. This, the less well known love-in-a-mist, has slightly wider leaves than its cousin and purple flowers that look as if they were painted with watercolors. Round buds and somewhat wrinkled sepals give a hint of the color. These sepals expand and provide a purple base for the almost invisible, gray-blue nectaries nearly hidden by red stamens and prominent bronze ovaries. The plant, though not as misty as *N. damascena*, is just as attractive.

The horned poppy, *Glaucium flavum*, grows but isn't allowed to bloom in the Dianthus Walk. Its cupped flower, yellow tinged with apricot, clashes with crim-

Nigella papillosa

Consolida ajacis (larkspur)

Glaucium flavum

Consolida ajacis

Achillea 'Moonshine'

son- and pink-flowered dianthus. I leave it there because the basal rosettes of silver-gray, deeply cut leaves provide a fine contrast to the many needle-leaved plants of dianthus and phlox. We let the poppy bloom in the scree and with love-in-a-mist, achillea, and larkspur in the Blue and Yellow Garden throughout June, and when the long curved seed pods ripen we collect the black seeds nestled in beige, cushioned beds.

The ground is as hard as a parking lot paved with concrete and most of our lawn is brown. The few patches of green come from pink- or white-flowered clover now blooming. I worry about my garden. About once a week during this severe drought we water the ash tree behind the house with water from the deep well. The next evening I water the largest, oldest white oak near the Rock Garden. In fact, I forgot one night and left the water running until five o'clock the next morning, when, dressed in my nightgown, I ran outside and turned off the pump to let the well recover enough water for the plants in pots. It isn't worth losing irreplaceable trees for the sake of a principle.

We had the deep well dug in the late 1980s to provide water for the nursery stock. At that time, I saw no end for Montrose Nursery, for it was gaining a reputation for offering unusual plants. Orders increased in size and quantity each year and I was excited about the future. We brought in a dowser who asked first where I wanted the well. I had a vague idea that it should be near the large greenhouse but said I could live with it anywhere as long as I had lots of water. I hoped for forty gallons a minute. A slender, slightly stooped man, about sixty years old, wandered around with two sticks and finally declared it should be dug near the big greenhouse right where I said I wanted it. I offered to pay him but he declined, saying his was a gift from God and therefore he couldn't charge anything for the use of his talent. He added that if I wanted to pay him something anyway, I could, and most people paid thirty-five dollars. I understood and paid.

The well digger worked for days, hitting water (five gallons a minute) at about one hundred and twenty-five feet, but he said he believed he was on the edge of a larger vein and recommended that we let him dig deeper. He went to six hundred feet and we still had five gallons a minute. He stopped digging and I cried. We pump water from that well all day whenever we have a drought and it has never yet gone dry. Either he tapped into a vein or created a large enough reservoir to supply most of our needs.

Every day the temperature remains below ninety degrees is a good day! We have more energy to plant the gardens, weed out nut sedge, and pot on tender decorative plants. We continued to plant, adding the reddest salvias to the red Color Garden, crocosmias to the Tropical Garden, and plectranthus to the shade area north of the Tropical Garden. This is a time of transition. We must wait for the seeds of late-spring annuals to ripen before we pull them out. And we can't plant summer annuals and tender perennials until we have that space. I am glad we have few visitors at this season. We need time to prepare for fall.

By late June we removed larkspur and nigella in the Blue and Yellow Garden, pulled off the ripe seeds sometimes in their capsules, and tossed them in all the bare spaces. It is amazing how much better a border looks after major editing. Deleting plants often makes a greater difference than adding new ones. We watered that garden thoroughly from the deep well in preparation for planting tender salvias and lantanas even though it will be a struggle to keep them alive until we get rain.

I organize every day, regardless of the season, around the weather reports. In the morning Craufurd and I hear at least two different versions of daily and weekly outlooks. At lunch I rush inside before 12:15 to hear a sequence of at least three and sometimes, if I am lucky, four versions of the approaching weather. In the evening we almost always hear four accounts. I always hope someone will predict rain.

By the end of the month we had cleared away the late-spring annuals and spring-flowering, heat-sensitive perennials from the Tropical Garden.

We pulled out calendulas, eschscholzias, and other poppies, collected seeds for next spring, and thinned the cannas. Then we removed the teepee that stood out like a wart in front of *Ligustrum quihoui*. Wayne Hall made this structure the year we tried to grow vegetables in the former stock area. It should have been the perfect support for climbing beans but the deer ate every leaf and bud.

The herd has come out of the woods now. I haven't seen a fawn yet, but the adults snort at me when I come to work in the law office. I feel a sense of despair when I look at our dry, nibbled garden. Woodchucks, known affectionately around here as "wood charleses," feed on dahlias, polygonatums, and even *Salvia sclarea*. Voles dig the bulbs in the Rock Garden at night. I am fighting back with cat litter. I accumulate the night's bounty and put it into a woodchuck's hole, or scatter it about where I have precious bulbs. I hope the scent will drive them away. I know the deer will grow bolder and bolder throughout the summer until, by August, they feast on the Dianthus Walk and Metasequoia Garden and sleep in the Rock Garden.

Brie's little dog, Cally, brightens our lives with her cheerful good humor. It doesn't matter that we don't know what breed she is, for she wags her tail and rolls over for a tummy rub whenever we greet her. After a few days of cautious curiosity, the cats have ignored her and now come over for pats whenever we rub the dog. One evening Cally and I went down to the nursery to collect plants for another urn and found Brie agitated after seeing a large blacksnake just beyond the nursery. I approached slowly, but Cally had delusions of bravery and went right up to the snake, which coiled and struck at her several times. The snake moved aggressively toward me. I merely wanted to drive him into the woods, but he faced me no matter where I stood. The dog and I shouted and our hero, Craufurd, approached to see who needed rescuing, at which point the snake slithered into the woods. I was sorry I missed seeing his escape, for nothing else moves with such fluid grace.

Gardenia jasminoides 'Radicans Variegata'

When I spent an afternoon in the woods garden pulling out microstegium along the Mother-in-Law Walk, I found a little moisture beneath the grass and thousands of young *Helleborus niger* seedlings. I worked on well-padded knees with a large nursery pot as weed bucket and heard only the sounds of birds and the occasional dash of a squirrel. In mid-afternoon I saw a black figure with pointed, triangular ears watching me from the bank. I first thought it was a piece of driftwood from the coast, now placed on an old stump, but couldn't remember that any part of it resembled ears. Then it moved. It was a scrawny little cat. I couldn't get any response from it and watched as it crept away.

Again I broke my resolve. This time I watered the Dianthus Walk. When I walked through that garden early one morning, all I could sense was the impending death of precious plants. Leaves curled back and flowers were scarce. The grass crunched when I walked on the lawn just as it does when frozen in winter. We are in the midst of a major drought.

Gardenia jasminoides 'Radicans Variegata' grows and blooms in a pot near the parking lot, where we have chairs and tables for those who wait for tours or for their companions to finish buying plants. It remains in a pot because gardenias aren't hardy at Montrose. Even 'Kleim's Hardy', a gardenia advertised as hardy to Zone 6, didn't survive a mild winter in my garden. Just a whiff of the flower's fragrance transported me to my old room in my parents' house, where a large plant grew below my bedroom window. We had no air conditioning so in summer

I slept on a daybed with my feet in an open window, lulled to sleep by the heavy, sweet scent of gardenias and the throbbing sounds of cicadas and tree frogs. We had an attic fan but my father wouldn't use it because, as he said, "it just stirs up hot air." I thought of my father's vegetable garden and the summer meals of tiny butter beans, sweet corn picked just before cooking, ripe tomatoes, okra, green beans, and country ham. A large gardenia grew beneath the kitchen window at Montrose when we moved here and we were told to look in the barn for a cover to protect it in winter. I don't garden like that and the plant died within several years.

The top leaves on the boxwoods, *Buxus sempervirens* 'Suffruticosa', in front of the house, are crisp and yellow. Although we have enough water left in the well at the end of the day to give each plant a fifteen-minute soak, I can't stay awake long enough to get to all of them. Boxwoods are important to this place. A plaque stating that Kathleen Long Graham rooted them beginning in 1927 is set in the final curve of the long serpentine border between a large Nordman fir and the north fence of the sunny gardens. These slow-growing shrubs have a naturally undulating shape and in fall spiders connect the branches with web terraces that catch the dew on cool mornings. I never prune, fertilize, or, until today, water them. I have continued the Graham tradition of propagating a few plants each year and now a circle of these younger boxwoods provides structural interest in winter in the Blue and Yellow Garden and a double row replaces a privet hedge that separates the lawn from a shady area for stock plants and leaf mulch.

JULY

In early July we felt desperate until one day clouds grew darker and we heard thunder. We ran into the potting room for safety and to avoid any chance of wasting a drop of rain on a person rather than on the ground. Drizzle became rain and finally a downpour left us with .34 of an inch. To celebrate we planted summer annuals and fertilized. We fertilize with Miracle-Gro all the pots and urns the first and third Monday of each month all summer. Although I found little moisture below the mulch after the shower, it gave me enormous pleasure to dig out a few of the tree seedlings that taunted me as I walked to the brush pile. Hellebores and pulmonarias remain so desiccated they lie flat against the ground.

The staff continued working in the heat when Craufurd and I went to Clint's memorial service. They reorganized the nursery, weeded, and repotted those plants in need of fresh soil and larger pots. Cheryl has assumed the responsibility for Jo's Bed, northeast of the lath house, and she added petunias, salvias, and *Catharanthus roseus* (annual vinca) to fill the gaps at the edge of the walk.

We planted Jo's Bed in 1993, a year after she died. Jo Petty came to work for me in 1987. She was in high school and called about three times asking whether I needed help. What would she do? I wondered. She would not know the plants well enough to weed and, even at that stage, I felt I didn't have time to teach her. After the third call, I decided to interview her. A young, slender girl with curly brown hair walked briskly but shyly toward me. I hired her immediately and never regretted it for a minute. She was an incredible worker who came nearly every day after school to wash pots and flats without a complaint. She set thousands of pots of nursery stock into the bark mulch where we overwintered them. When her friend Paula Brinegar joined her on the staff, they worked happily together, laughing and talking. After Jo went away to college, she returned to help during every break and for much of each summer. I can hear her now: "Mrs. Goodwin, this is Jo. Do you have anything for me to do?"

I will never forget the telephone call received on Sunday, July 19, 1992, about a month before her twentieth birthday. "Jo was in an automobile accident. It was fatal." She had driven onto Highway 70 in front of her house, was struck by a bus, and killed instantly. We arranged flowers from the garden for the funeral to which the entire staff went. I cannot remember a sadder occasion.

I wanted a tangible, daily reminder of Jo, so planted and dedicated a garden to her. Although her border comes to a peak in late summer with lespedezas, buddlejas, and altheas, we enjoy the fragrance of the banana shrub, *Michelia figo,* in early spring; we have roses in May; *Ruellia brittoniana*, rain and crinum lilies in early summer; and our best beautyberry, *Callicarpa bodinieri* 'Profusion', in fall. A small plaque with Jo's dates is set in the front of the path in the middle of her garden. Her mother, Dot Petty, a good friend, visits the garden on Jo's birth and death dates, at Christmas, Mother's Day, and at unexpected times throughout the year. We speak of Jo. She tells of

In Memory
Johanna Gay Petty

August 18, 1972
July 19, 1998

places she remembers finding her working in the garden and I talk of Jo's sweet nature and incredible work ethic.

Jo's death was a turning point in my life. I thought of the tragedy of Jo's short life and all of the wonderful experiences she never had. After lengthy discussions with Craufurd, I decided to give up my lucrative nursery and devote the remainder of my life to making and maintaining this garden. I announced the closing of the mail-order nursery in the next spring catalog and 1993 was our final year to ship plants.

When we moved here in 1977 there was a cold frame on the site of Jo's Bed. It was made of concrete blocks, stacked two deep little more than a foot below ground level, and had a storm door hinged onto a wooden support with a fastener at the back for protection on cold nights. I was curious about the structure but had no idea how to use it, so called the Agricultural Extension Service for advice, but no one there knew anything about managing a cold frame. I was excited about making a garden at Montrose that first spring, and ordered seeds of many of the plants I had grown successfully in Durham. As soon as a pot of seeds germinated, I placed it in the bottom of the cold frame and had the best luck ever in producing strong young seedlings. I quickly realized why. Most seedlings grow best with cold air in full sun. Miraculously, slugs never entered that structure the first year. The potential danger of a cold frame was a frightening discovery. The weather was cold and cloudy at one point during that first spring so I didn't open the frame for two days. When I did, on the third morning, I discovered Impy, our little gray tabby cat, eager to escape. That third day saw temperatures into the nineties, which she couldn't have survived. When we made Jo's memorial garden, we removed the old cold frame.

The little shower brought rain lilies into flower as if on command. They might have bloomed even if it hadn't rained, but the flowers would have been smaller. *Habranthus robustus*, with flowers in shades of pink and white,

Habranthus robustus

looks fresh and cool even on this, one of the hottest days thus far this summer. Ippy drew one. She is now a part of our team. I don't expect to see her weeding or planting but I love seeing her with her large straw hat, intent on capturing the essence of some plant or place.

June bugs emerged along with the rain lilies and hovered about a foot above ground, buzzing and bumping into us and the walls of the buildings, and falling into the rain containers. We watched as several came up head first from below ground for the first time. These, the youngest beetles, were brilliant iridescent green, much brighter than they will be after a day's exposure to light and sun. My brother, sister, and I used to love to catch June bugs when we were children. We thought it an act of enormous bravery to hold a beetle with wildly groping legs.

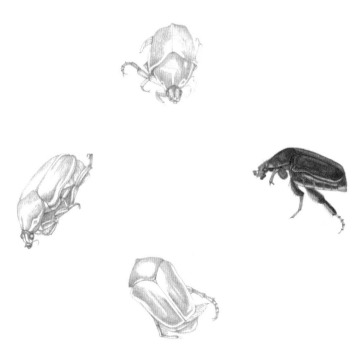

Most of the staff were away the first week of July and it took more than half of each day to water recently planted salvias and solenostemons, pots and urns, and nursery stock. For four days we cleared off the lath house. Pruning roses is a job for two people so Brie and I tackled it. A blanket of rose canes covered many layers of dead branches, now hard but not brittle enough to break away easily. Roses 'Bobbie James', 'The Garland', 'Alexandre Girault', 'Madame Alfred Carrière', 'Léontine Gervais', 'American Beauty', 'François Juranville', and 'Madame Grégoire Staechelin' had grown layer upon layer of long thorny canes, and little light reached the ground beneath. The dense accumulation of dead roses and vines caused the decline of the garden below. Little rain penetrates it now and the plants are suffering. I feel like I am about to restore the secret garden.

I worried about being on the top of the structures, now fifteen years old, and I am afraid of ladders. In fact, I thought I would never manage to step off the ladder onto the slats at the top of the lath house, even though I had watched Wayne and Ron build it and walk with confidence across the beams. Nor did I think I would have the courage to get back onto the ladder even if I had stepped off it. I conquered both fears and by the end of a week went up and down the ladder holding tools and a water bottle in one hand. I crawled across the top of the structure with careful confidence. Brie worked on a ladder at the base and we cut away much new growth and all the old dead canes. We removed much of the variegated elaeagnus, *Elaeagnus pungens* 'Maculata', on the roof of the building, and espaliered the remaining branches on its north side. We found intricate small birds' nests and one large messy one, with a basket-like base of nursery labels. I was relieved not to find any wasps' nests.

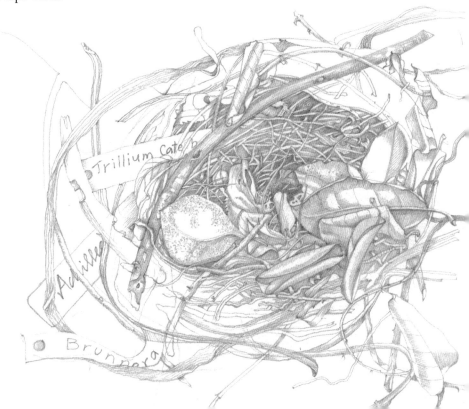

We hauled load after load of clippings into the woods and, with many groans and two pitchforks, threw them together onto the top of a brush pile. We gave ourselves gold, silver, or no medal depending on the size of the load and how far we threw it into the center of the pile. We were dirty and bloody, and covered with rose debris in our hair and on our clothes. We laughed as we worked and, as we grew tired, giggled when we couldn't lift even a small load. At the end of each day's labor we estimated how many more days it would take to finish clearing the lath house.

The lath house is the most beautiful trellis on the property. An arbor covered with scuppernong grapes was on this site when we moved here. Every January for our first seven years I pruned the vines and every September Craufurd and I made wine. The wine, a sweet but powerful dessert wine, wasn't very good. The first time we made it we went into the woods to the old dump and pulled out the bottles the Grahams used, sterilized them, and filled them with our wine. The entire house smelled of fermenting grapes for weeks. We still have a few bottles left in the basement and I half expect the house to rise from its foundation when they all explode. Perhaps we shouldn't have put new wine in old bottles.

Record-breaking cold in the winter of 1985 killed our camellias to the ground and killed the grapes completely. The arbor on which they grew was in bad condition so two years later we commissioned Wayne Hall to design and build a lath house. By that time my nursery had expanded beyond the production of cyclamen, boxwood, and primroses and I needed a place to grow special hellebores, tiarellas, primroses, and other shade-loving plants for propagation by division instead of seed. A trellis would enable me to grow and control roses, honeysuckles, and the climbing aster, *Aster carolinianus*. I knew I could grow plants well here away from tree roots.

Wayne's design was based on the roof lines of the old smokehouse, barn, and law office. The building is forty-eight feet long, twenty-four feet wide, and twenty-one feet high at its highest point, making it the focal point of the sunny gardens. Wayne created half shade by alternating a wood slat with an equal amount of space. A steeply pointed roof supported by an arch covers the widest path, from north to south, through the building. When viewing it from east or west, we look through three arches, the central one of which frames the Albert memorial at the western edge of the garden. Several years ago Wayne set a sixty-gallon iron pot into the ground beneath the center of the structure. In summer we keep that pot filled with water and add a little pump that creates a soft gurgling sound. When I am in the center of the lath house garden, I feel as if I am in a cathedral. The air beneath the slatted roof is cooler, the soil damper than in surrounding gardens, and the scale of the structure so large it makes me feel insignificant.

Brie called in with a temperature the week after we began our mammoth pruning task. I expressed concern, and couldn't stop worrying about her. "Rocky Mountain spotted fever," I thought, "and it is all my fault." Earlier this spring Cathy got the disease from a tick at her farm, and I knew we had seen several ticks during the past few weeks. Although I have insect repellent in the potting room, and encourage everyone to use it, I realize it isn't 100 percent effective. I insisted that she see a doctor right away. Several hours later she called with the diagnosis—severe dehydration. We drink copious amounts of cold water, but that wasn't enough for her. I am both relieved by the diagnosis and concerned that we don't know how much we need to drink.

We planted the bank below the sunny gardens with

Tiarella wherryi

yuccas shortly after I closed my nursery. Few people bought my beautiful *Yucca smalliana*. Rather than discard the plants, we set them into a bank between the sunny gardens and the woods. We added a few young plants of *Rhus michauxii*, presents from J. C. Raulston. I was eager to grow this rare sumac with brown, furry stems, an inflorescence of many tiny, pale beige and green flowers, and fall leaves in shades of yellow and red. This species has a wandering nature and has gone throughout the length and width of the bed and into the lawn. In a normal summer we seldom see plants outside the bed because Craufurd mows them regularly, but this summer he mows the tufts of weeds and grass once a month or less. The sumac thrives on little moisture, no fertilizer, and no mowing. During July we cleared the Yucca Bank, removing unwanted trees and a pesky verbesina. That verbesina, *V. alternifolia*, has a woody root system, unattractive, mustard yellow flowers with few ray petals, and seeds that germinate readily. I cannot pull it up and must use a spade or fork to dig every plant. Its attractive, annual cousin, *V. encelioides*, is welcome in the Blue and Yellow Garden where its bright yellow, daisy-like flowers are an important feature during summer.

A cool week meant we worked in comfort even in the sun. Cathy has charge of the garden on the west side of the law office. That garden has always been a challenge for me—a challenge not met until now. When we moved here, *Hydrangea macrophylla*, mop-headed hydrangeas, interplanted with the brightest yellow-flowering *Forsythia* x *intermedia*, grew on two sides of the building. I moved the forsythia to the edge of the pond where I had visions of its reflected glory in the spring. Beavers destroyed every plant within a year. The hydrangeas went onto the brush pile to live only in memory. I planted an oak leaf hydrangea, *H. quercifolia*, from my mother-in-law's garden. At one end of the west facing border I began a little purple and orange border, with an orange polyantha rose given to me by a piano student, orange 'Connecticut Yankee' lilies, and dark purple-blue *Salvia* x *sylvestris* 'May Night' ['Mainacht']. This little planting inspired the Tropical Garden a decade later. I added a few slow-growing shrubs that have become trees, alas. *Chamaecyparis pisifera* 'Boulevard' rises above the corner of the building and a massive *Corylopsis sinensis* var. *calvescens* f. *veitchiana* matches the blue-needled cypress in height but surpasses it in girth. We prune both severely each spring to keep them in bounds. Every year we remove large branches from the weeping youpon holly, *Ilex vomitoria* 'Pendula', to keep it away from the old building. This year Cathy planted dark burgundy and chartreuse solenostemons, *Salvia blepharophylla*, New Guinea hybrid impatiens, and *Rumex flexuosus* in front of this shrubby green background and finally turned it into an exciting late summer garden. She also revised the

Rosa 'Mary Wallace'

little garden near the pump house using similar colors but more drought-resistant plants — verbenas in place of solenostemons.

We spent another week on roses. First we battled *R.* 'Albéric Barbier', which had traveled east and west along the fence and over an entrance to the sunny gardens. I had removed its mate from the shrub border two years ago because it smothered everything in its path. I thought I could control this one, and I think so again, now that we have given it major surgery and a crew cut. Taming *R.* 'Doctor W. Van Fleet' was our next task and we cut out the dead and oldest canes, and wove the remaining ones into the fence. Our greatest challenge was the peak of the main entrance to the Tropical Garden. Shortly after Wayne completed the lath house, he designed and built a fence to replace the old cedar post-and-wire one. He constructed the new fence of the same material that formed the lath house and made three entrances on the north side of the former kitchen gardens, now our main sunny gardens. He made the widest our primary entrance, in line with the north-south passage through the lath house. Its peaked roof and arch match those that frame the big urn in the axis of the paths in the Color Gardens. The angle of this roof matches that on the oldest part of the law office. *R.* 'Mary Wallace,' on both sides of the entrance, is a primary feature of our garden in May when covered with semi-double, medium pink flowers. This rambunctious rose has large, stiff thorns and an aggressive nature. We began at the edges and, after a day's labor, opened a passage high enough for one of us to climb onto the roof of the entrance. All the next day we worked slowly, with many exclamations of pain and bloody arms and legs, and cut out the dead canes and pulled away the young vigorous growth of the old rose. Finally we rewove the pliable young shoots back through the slats of the entranceway. Although I think we are tackling the hardest roses first, we find each rose more difficult than the last. Certainly *R.* 'Mary Wallace' fought us every step of the way. When we pruned the large Cherokee roses, *R. laevigata*, on one of Wayne's finest arbors, the semi-circular one in the May Garden, we wove the rose canes into the primary and secondary ribs of the arbor. Next we tackled *R.* 'Silver Moon'. I had dreaded it because I remember the year that rose brought down its support, a teepee, similar to the one we removed from the Tropical Garden. Long, thorny canes had grown out from the base in all directions and I couldn't get near enough to prune it so Wayne installed a square of juniper posts outside the first structure. This time we went at 'Silver Moon' from all sides, cutting old canes to the ground, and weaving the most pliable, younger ones through the main supports.

Our final two roses were an unknown yellow one with small, stiff, and hurtful thorns and *R.* 'Albertine'. *R.* 'Albertine' has been a part of my garden for years. I first received it as a gift for our Durham garden because the donor found it unmanageable. I planted it in the lower section of our property where it grabbed at Craufurd when he mowed near it. Too vigorous, I thought, and gave it to my father, who took it for his garden. The rose had spread in an unwieldy way over eight feet. My father cut each stalk about a foot above the base of the plant, pulled away the vicious canes, and dug the root easily and quickly. After we moved to Hillsborough, I thought I had room and knowledge enough to deal with *R.* 'Albertine' so I asked for a cutting only to discover that he, too, had found it impossible to live with. I bought a new plant that now grows under one of Wayne's beautiful arbors. Finally it is under control.

I know why this is the perfect time to prune roses. Although we weren't completely comfortable working in sleeveless shirts and shorts, we were careful and saw every rose make a fresh spurt of growth shortly after pruning. New shoots on the first plants we pruned grew more than a foot within a month. Plants clamber through fences and arbors and the structures that support them are visible again. Although we will continue to tuck in new canes as they grow long enough, we won't prune again until next summer. We have revealed the essence of Wayne's work by using vines and plants to enhance rather than conceal his trellises.

Rosa 'Silver Moon'

We set four traps baited with carrots for the woodchucks. This land is not just for people and we try to tolerate the creatures who live here with us. We don't hunt or allow anyone else to hunt the deer. We coexist with rabbits and foxes. I believe we had a bear pass through here in the mid-1990s. We found our garbage cans moved about fifty feet from the back door. Large stumps in the woods were pulled out of the ground and I saw scat unlike any I had ever seen before. Cindy, one of our cats, disappeared for a week and returned a frightened creature. During the past few years our woodchuck population has multiplied and as it has, the devastation in the garden has increased. These rodents with insatiable appetites will eat almost everything. The day's growth in one of the Color Gardens is eaten each night. Dahlias are stomped and chomped. I spread cat excrement and put bamboo sticks around the plants in the black and red planter. Nothing worked. So the traps are my declaration of war. If I don't catch a woodchuck the first night, I will add bits of apple and other vegetables to each trap. I won't give up until I discover their favorite vegetable, fruit, or candy. I will even let them eat cake.

Craufurd spent several weeks rescuing the junipers near the fence between us and Cameron Park Elementary School. Grape, poison ivy, and honeysuckle had grown to the top of some of the trees and smaller tree seedlings were tall enough to challenge the older conifers for light. The drought gives him time to do this now that he does little mowing. Tree seedlings in the fields are about eight inches high. Small persimmons grow in the lawn next to the nursery and blackberry brambles have spilled out from our blackberry patch and now grow in the adjacent field. The next mowing will take care of them, but it frightens me to realize how quickly we might revert to forest.

Eryngium
ebracteatum

Heat returned in mid-month but we continued planting, adding more gomphrenas and marigolds to the Tropical Garden. We have nearly finished the summer gardens, and, from now on, will fill in gaps, and correct our mistakes by deleting plants that clash with their neighbors. Two eryngiums bloom in the Burgundy and Silver Garden, the southeast quadrant of the Color Gardens. Both have silver foliage but the newer one in this garden, *E. ebracteatum*, has slender leaves and burgundy inflorescences held like a delicate candelabra above the base. *E. yuccifolium*, rattlesnake-master, has broader leaves, more like a yucca's, and a silvery knob of flowers. I can only guess at the origin of the common name, but a glance confirms the appropriateness of its botanical one. The leaves really do make the plant look like a yucca.

Eryngium yuccifolium

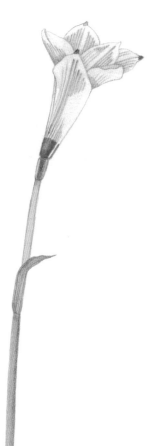

Blue habranthus

The blue habranthus bloomed last weekend. This flower, though not pure blue, is smoky blue tinged with pink. This is a major moment in our rain lily season, for I have never read of a habranthus that color nor seen one except here. I ordered seeds from a seed exchange as "Rain lily collected in Mexico." This ambiguous description was enough to tempt me, so about ten years ago I planted five seeds that germinated quickly. This species doesn't bloom unless I keep it bone dry from May until July, when I set the pots on the porch. Neither tap water nor well water brings the plants into flower but rain seems to produce them as if by magic.

I had a brief but delightful reprieve celebrating the birthdays of two good friends. It has been a long time since I took a break from the garden in mid-day to enjoy the civilized pleasures of good food, wine, and stimulating talk. When I returned after lunch, I found Roger and Tony intent on some creature. Further inspection revealed a tiny bunny with a small white mark on his forehead. I rescued him and called for help. I was also holding the mail, a handbag, and a package. Craufurd came with the bird box from the potting room. About that time, we found another little rabbit, and shortly thereafter a third one. I called animal control and was told that the rabbits, now four inches long, could probably survive on their own if I release them into a thicket. We took them to the pond where we set them free in the heavy brush near the spillway. I know rabbits do much damage to my garden but I can't resist those little creatures. Just before dinner,

Tony cornered the fourth one near the back door and I took him to the briar patch near the nursery. I hope they all have long and happy lives down in the woods, well away from the temptations of the gardens near the house.

It was the middle of the month before we finished pruning the roses on the fence that separates the lawn and Boxwood Border from the sunny gardens. When we carried our last loads of rose clippings to the brush pile, we looked like neglected, homeless people, with torn clothes, scratches on our arms and legs, and hot, sweaty bodies. We were so happy! After we threw the final load onto the top of the brush pile, we gave ourselves life-time achievement awards. We did not puncture a single tire on the carts we used to haul our prunings. We made the piles higher, not broader. We did not fall off a ladder or the roof of any structure. We didn't kill a rose. What more is there?

That accomplished, we turned our attention to sections of the gardens not yet planted for fall. We planted the Bank with drought-tolerant salvias, ballotas, yuccas, and calaminthas from the stock area. First we soaked the entire bed, then set in the plants, and soaked it again. We will water the newly planted areas each day for several weeks or until it rains. In past years, that meant a week or two. This year, it may mean months. I still water everything we planted this summer in the May Garden and Aster Border.

Our hot, humid, unhealthy air is taking a toll on the staff. Now three employees have been ill from heat exhaustion. The problem arises because each of us wants to complete the tasks she begins each day. Cheryl became ill after planting rain lilies in the Circle Garden, Cathy after finishing her new plantings around the pump house and law office, and Brie after mulching the entire lath house the day we finished pruning the roses. Craufurd bought us sports drinks with electrolytes to replace those we lose each day. It is no fun being the employer. I must always assume the burden of guilt.

Late in the afternoon of July 19, Mrs. Petty came to visit Jo's Bed as she

has for ten years on this special, sad day. Although that garden was not at a peak, it had some flowers, including rain lilies, *Lycoris squamigera* (resurrection lilies), x *Amarcrinum memoria-corsii* 'Howardii', and *Hibiscus syriacus* (altheas).

The roses, pruned so severely earlier this month, showed signs of recovery by the middle of the month. Healthy new shoots, some four inches long, appeared all along the new canes. Although it will probably take another week or two for the plants on the fence to grow, I know they will and the plants will look natural by Garden Open Day in September. Ferns beneath the lath house have fresh new fronds, and perky young plants of *Arisaema candidissimum* responded to the additional light.

We added *Leonotis leonurus* and more bananas to the Tropical Garden and then revised the southeast end of the Boxwood Border. This section east of the boxwoods was the first garden I planted at Montrose. During August of that hot, dry summer in 1977, I barely explored the grounds. I was intent on organizing the house. When rain softened the soil in early fall, I returned to my former garden on Cranford Road in Durham and dug out some of the plants marked before we put the house and garden on the market. I filled the back of the 1961 Apache Chevrolet truck we purchased with this property and brought only one load of treasures. Every time I dug a hole for one of my precious plants from Durham, I heard a sickening crunch as I cut into bulbs, so I selected a strip of land beside a path in the old kitchen garden and heeled in shrubs to wait for permanent homes until the bulbs emerged in spring and I knew the garden better. Many of those plants grow there still in the garden now named the Cranford Road Bed.

The first winter at Montrose was cold and snowy. Carpenters and painters worked inside and outside the house for months. I had no kitchen. On the first day of spring the temperature rose to seventy degrees and I could wait no longer. Craufurd tilled the lawn next to the boxwoods and I planted daisies, phloxes, bergamot, and other perennials from Mother's garden. I sowed seeds of summer annuals. I planted a vitex to replace the one too large to move from the Durham garden, and put a little rooted piece of my old *Hydrangea paniculata* 'Tardiva' at the south end of the bed. Everything grew like the books said it would. I wasn't used to that. Nothing in my first garden grew like the books promised. The Hillsborough dirt—loamy clay, rich in minerals—lived up to its reputation. In July, the first phase of house improvement was complete and we had a party. Craufurd said I must not cut a single flower; it would spoil the entire garden. I was thrilled!

Twenty-five years later those phloxes have grown into thick clumps and

seeded about, and now they are a mess. First we dug out about three-quarters of them—those with poor colors. In their places we planted salvias: *S. mexicana* 'Limelight', *S. guaranitica* 'Late Blooming Giant', *S. x jamensis* 'Raspberry Royale', *S. involucrata* 'Mulberry Jam', and *S.* 'Indigo Spires'. We put petunias and verbenas at the edge of the bed, and the purple-stemmed grass, *Setaria palmifolia*, at the south end. *Pennisetum setaceum* 'Burgundy Giant' filled the gaps toward the middle of the bed.

A velvet ant came scurrying by as we planted. We put this creature with bright red, velvety patches separated by black bands into a container for Ippy to draw. I vaguely remembered that it isn't an ant at all but wasn't certain what it is until Ippy discovered that the velvet ant, also known as cow killer, is a female, wingless wasp. A large blacksnake slithered from the rose-covered fence into the May Garden, and we found a large, gray sphinx moth on the *Buddleja crispa* that we were about to plant. The moth, with yellow stripes on its body, and black markings on its head, must have emerged recently from its cocoon, for, as we watched, and Ippy drew, the wings expanded and by the end of the afternoon it had evolved into a fully developed moth. When I was ready to put away my tools, it crept beneath the cart and, fearing I would run over it, I put down a finger for it to climb to safety. It must have felt very safe or perhaps curious, for it crept all over my shirt and I removed it to a barberry with difficulty.

Saturday lunches are special. Ippy, Craufurd, and I are usually the only ones here so we have bacon, lettuce, and tomato sandwiches and wine together. The tomatoes are ripe and plentiful at the farmers' market. I am always so hot and dirty I must sit on a large towel draped over my chair. We all return to work, happy, relaxed, and as refreshed as possible in ninety-degree weather.

Late in the month we added nepetas (*N.* 'Six Hills Giant' and *N. racemosa* 'Walker's Low') to the Circle Garden and then planted *Penstemon* 'Evelyn' and seedling *Clematis integrifolia* from my best and largest-flowered plants. We hope the nepetas will protect the clematis from predators. Hauling hoses, Plantone (my favorite organic fertilizer), and carts filled with tools everywhere we went, we put salvias, lantanas, verbenas, and pennisetums in all the sunny gardens. We watered as we planted, and we watered again at the end of each day.

Showery rain fell in refreshing spurts for two days and left a little more than an inch in total. The lawn is greener already so we mulched newly planted areas and most of the sunny gardens to conserve this precious moisture and had our first relaxed afternoon in the potting room listening to music while we divided saxifrages and potted up cyclamen. Bonnie resigned to pursue a career in garden design.

The potting room, built about 1830, is the original kitchen for the property. Because it is about a hundred yards from the main house, we imagine the nineteenth-century Grahams had many cold dinners prepared there. More recently the building was Mr. Alexander H. (Sandy) Graham's work-

room. His sons, John and Sandy Graham, from whom we purchased Montrose, did not clean out the buildings before we moved in. We agreed to that, hoping and expecting to find treasures as we explored the contents of each place. When Craufurd began to turn this former kitchen into his workroom, he glanced up at the ceiling and saw in a corner of the building a square surrounded by lines. When he poked the area with a pole, it moved. He had found the "secret" entrance to the second floor. We went up on a ladder and discovered a bed, some "Sandy Graham for Governor" signs, but no Confederate money. Around 1988 Wayne converted the lower room into a potting room for the nursery staff. The building has one large room downstairs with a fireplace originally used for cooking. A simple ladder must have led to the second floor where the cook slept. Wayne built sturdy stairs to replace the ladder and put in sister beams next to the old ones to support the second floor, where we store pots and fertilizer. He painted the wood gray and the walls white, and we added a small propane gas heater for winter use and a fan for summer. There is a table in the center of the room with three large potting benches against the walls with fluorescent lights above each. We have a refrigerator, originally to store seeds, but now also to hold staff lunches, water, and an occasional bottle of wine. A microwave oven on top of the refrigerator means the staff can have hot meals in winter, and a radio on the east-facing bench provides music while we work. We keep potting soil, coarse perlite, granite grit, sand, and seed-starting soil in containers on the floor. The location of the benches means we usually work facing the windows or walls and have wonderful conversations. Talking while moving hands removes most inhibitions.

Directly south of this building a shallow, stone-lined well, probably dug by hand, produces only a gallon and a half of water per minute — just enough to water in newly potted plants. We installed an old sink found in the barn, for pre-washing dirt-covered hands. A continuous roof connects the kitchen and well to a smaller food storage building, where we keep boxes for nursery sales. Craufurd collects most of them from dumpsters and from friends on the Duke campus. The seed-germinating dungeon is on the west side of this building.

A large grove of unidentified fig trees, really shrubs, grows between the garage and potting room. We know only what they aren't — 'Brown Turkey' or 'Celeste'. On the garage side they grow in raised beds where the Grahams must have covered them with plastic in winter. Even though we don't protect them, they are so large by summer's end we cannot walk between the buildings. In severe winters the plants are killed to the ground, but by early fall they always produce a large, luscious crop of fruit.

The recent rain and new growth on the grass forced Craufurd to mow for the first time in months. The vessels beneath the barn roof edge finally filled with water and more rain lilies bloomed. The Dianthus Walk is cheerful with bright yellow *Zephyranthes citrina* on the west side and paler yellow *Z. smallii* on the east. The latter opens wide from a clear yellow bud to reveal six tepals in two sets of three, and it remains open at night. Because this species doesn't increase below ground, I sow every seed. Collecting seeds, even from a pot, isn't as easy as one might imagine, for we have creatures that go onto the front porch to feast on them the night they ripen.

AUGUST

We survived July. Signs of fall are seen but not felt. *Cyclamen hederifolium* and *Leucojum autumnale* (fall snowflake) bloom in increasing numbers and the garden under the deodara cedar near the front door looks misty with hundreds of spikes of purple scillas, *Scilla autumnalis*, carpeting the earth beneath. Flowers that were barely visible in early morning fluff out by late afternoon. Thick, heavy, hazy days of late summer deny the approach of fall. I will never get used to it, but endure it year after year without feeling sorry for myself. We may have a few cool, clear days in August, and September is next.

August 4 marks the twenty-fifth anniversary of our coming to Montrose. We knew then that living in this place would be the adventure of our lives and Craufurd and I were excited. Even though we had not actually closed on the property, the Grahams let us move in, as guardians rather than owners. John gave us the keys to the house—hundreds and hundreds of them. We later learned that the nineteenth-century leather key box, which held the essential keys, was a gift from Paul Carrington Cameron to his daughter, Rebecca, when she married John W. Graham in 1867. They also gave us a large paper sack half full of keys. There were keys to "the white face pasture," to chests of drawers and small boxes, to every room in the house and law office, and to almost every door in every building on the property. I resolved to match each key to its lock, and although I haven't done that yet, we still have every single key. We loaded the old green pickup truck with our essential belongings and I brought my parents over for their first inspection. Although they had seen the garden, they had not seen the interior of any building or the rest of the land.

We returned to Durham, brought over a second load of furniture and our two cats, Thomas and Jane Welsh, and slept the first night on mattresses on

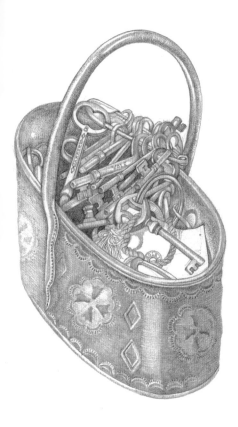

the floor. For about a week, we brought load after load of possessions in our new old truck and at the end of the week professional movers brought the piano, harpsichord, and heaviest furniture. Each night after supper we wandered about the property exploring the buildings, the garden, and the land. The place didn't feel like it belonged to us. When we looked over toward St. Matthew's Episcopal Church, where many of the Grahams are buried, we wondered what they would think. We weren't kissing kin; none of them had even heard of us. We first met the Hillsborough Grahams when we came to consider buying the property.

How much longer will this drought last? It began five years ago in 1998 when Allen Lacy and I were in the midst of our correspondence. I tried to describe for him the feeling of desperation I had at that time, but was afraid of boring him with the most salient features of that summer—unrelenting heat, humidity, and drought. The monotony of the weather that year made each day more painful than the last. I was optimistic then, for I believed that would remain the most awful summer of my gardening life. Little did I know that, five years later, I would once again try to describe the delights and challenges of this garden, only to find that we are still under that same oppressive umbrella of heat and dryness, and that this summer is even worse. Little has changed except the pond, which is down by three or four feet. I have watched, with despair, many young trees and a few old ones die. When the town first requested voluntary water restrictions, they asked that residents water no trees or

shrubs, but allowed them to water "ornamental" plants. They should have allowed them to water trees and shrubs first. Ornamental plants are easily replaced. Cooler nights and rain are necessary for the garden to reach this year's climax, and, although we will certainly have the former, I wonder whether we will have the latter. I no longer believe this will be the most awful summer. Next summer may be worse still.

One evening in early August the wind shifted to the northwest and cool, clear, Canadian air blew in without a storm. Craufurd and I walked through the garden after dinner. The sun had set and our garden was filled with soft gray light that hides defects and enhances all silver, yellow, gray, and white objects. Two cats—Tony, our gray tabby, and Beanie, a tuxedo one, with black and white fur—accompanied us. We sat on the fern bench beneath the recently pruned rose and looked down the path to the bathtub, the urn planted with rose-pink, silver, and gray foliage and pink, white, and purple flowers, while Tony rolled in the gravel and Beanie sat on the bench with us. The summer garden is beginning to come together now. Buddlejas,

Lilium formosanum

vitex, lantanas, *Lilium formosanum*, and *Ceratotheca triloba* with white flowers form soft glowing mounds and green, purple, and pink disappear in the night light.

We seldom sit in the garden. For one thing, I can't relax enough to ignore the weeds around me. I want to walk slowly and criticize the plantings, search for ailing plants, and decide how each section can be better. Craufurd always has work to do inside — a book or an article to read or write. This was a rare treat, for we walked together unaccompanied by mosquitoes, deer, or woodchucks. The ground is so hard we have no moles but we do have webworms. Pecans, persimmons, and other fruit trees look festive with silvery webs clothing their branches. Caterpillars ate many leaves but left nuts or fruit on bare branches.

Craufurd and I have joyous meetings with Cally each morning as she runs to greet us, moaning and getting lower

Persimmon with webs

Cally

and lower, as she approaches, finally rolling on her back in submission. Her feet are her best feature. Curly hair makes them more appropriate for a super cocker spaniel. A delightful little animal with manners, she begs for food with her eyes, and doesn't show her resentment at every bite we take, the way our labrador did. She accepts gently anything offered.

We received a large shipment of potting soil early in the month. It has been a challenge to find the best soil to use in pots. The commercial mixture used successfully in the early days of Montrose Nursery is no longer available, so I tried making my own potting soil by mixing bark and sand with peat and coarse perlite. The sand contained weed seeds that produced bumper crops of vigorous little seedlings that rapidly went to seed. Weeding the stock required a full-time person. At one time I microwaved dirt to sterilize it and amended it with perlite but the plants didn't grow well in that either. Besides, I don't have time to cook dirt every day nor do I want to sell at any price this good Orange County soil. Our new product comes in heavy bags and we carried each bag from the truck to our storage area and covered it with black plastic. I will know later whether I have found the best solution.

By the end of the second week in August we had nearly finished planting the garden for fall. Designing the summer garden seems to take forever. When sections aren't quite right, the solution more often comes to me while I am lying in bed, rather than when I'm standing in front of the problem. I have a memory of past gardens that possibly never were as wonderful as I now imagine and a mental image of those yet unbloomed, recently acquired plants. I consider myself an editor rather than a designer. The gardens here have evolved slowly, each with its own character, color scheme, or peak time. They are more similar to musical compositions than to paintings. I begin each section with an idea of form (the shape of the bed and arrangement of plants within it), color (the underlying theme and search for harmony), quality of site (moisture, soil type), year-round structure (trees, shrubs, hedges or built trellises), purpose (to block or enhance another view), and season of primary interest. Secondary considerations include neighboring beds, the remainder of the year, and maintenance requirements.

Maintenance is the last consideration. If the idea is worth trying, I can figure out how to maintain it. I have, however, never been tempted to have a bog garden, except in pots without drainage holes. I have to fight my reluctance to move plants that don't harmonize with their neighbors. These are often plants that died elsewhere, plants that I wanted for years, or those that are rare or difficult. A healthy, well-grown plant, wherever it is, gives the greatest pleasure. Sometimes design factors prompt a move but more often I live with a little dissonance.

Experiencing the garden is like hearing or performing music. A garden is a living, constantly evolving composition impossible to freeze in time. It can neither be hurried nor held back but develops slowly, so slowly that often the changes are barely discernible. Each part may turn out as hoped for only once. If I happen to see (or hear) it, it is thrilling, but if I don't, I may not recapture the moment. It is never again the same; it is impossible to control.

I purchased a *Magnolia stellata* the first year here in hopes of recreating a bit of my old Durham garden. My small plant, from a reputable nursery, went into the Paisley Border; in fact I planned the whole garden around it.

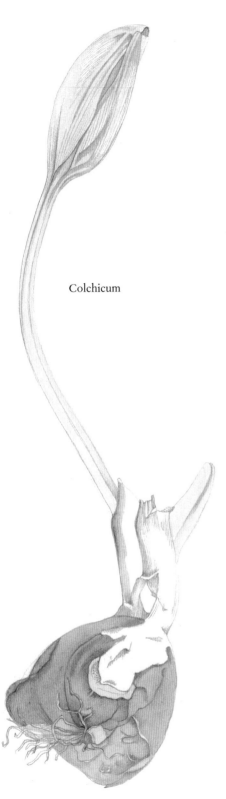

Colchicum

I thought it would bloom early in spring, occasionally just before a devastating frost, but I expected the buds to open more often to a frazzle of white, twisted, slightly fragrant petals. Nearby I planted an orange-scarlet sport of my favorite red-flowering quince, *Chaenomeles* x *superba* 'Crimson and Gold' from my old garden. I went further and developed a warm color scheme with yellow, burnt orange, and near-red butterfly weeds, *Asclepias tuberosa*, bright orange *Lychnis cognata* and *Geum* 'Mrs. J. Bradshaw', and shrubby *Hypericum* 'Hidcote' (St. John's wort) with bright yellow powder puff flowers. Each spring I anticipated the flowers on my magnolia, and for ten years was disappointed. I thought the new plant would be superior to my old one because it grew taller, less shrub-like. After ten years my magnolia, then taller than I imagined it could be, bloomed with the darkest magenta-purple flowers I had ever seen. "It looks a little French," I thought. But never once did I think it beautiful in combination with the orange-red quince. Because the tree was too large to transplant, I removed the quince and left the remaining warm-color plants because they bloom after the magnolia, now identified as *M. liliflora* 'Nigra'.

The Paisley Border, formerly a star-shaped bed of lilies-of-the-valley, *Convallaria majalis*, was planted by my predecessor, Mrs. Graham. She so loved these plants that she gave a party each spring when they bloomed. She filled the house with them and draped bunches on the sides of her damask tablecloth. The star shape of the bed had disappeared by the time we arrived but the lilies-of-the-valley remained so I kept the bed and gave up any hope of restoring its star shape. It was by then a round bed. When I connected the bed to my seedling *Magnolia macrophylla* to the north, the border formed a paisley shape, hence the name.

Two colchicums bloom at the edge of the woods in late August. They even bloom on store shelves without soil or moisture. Hybrid lycoris bloom in pots in the shady cold frames. They have no excuse not to bloom for we watered them diligently all summer. Soft apricot-yellow flowers on *L.* 'Hill Beyond Hill' look pristine and cool like chiffon or sherbet. Four flowers at the top of a stiff stalk face outward with slightly curled stamens and a pink, protruding stigma.

Lycoris 'Hill Beyond Hill'

Although most asters and many salvias won't bloom until mid-September, others are in full bloom. Cat's whiskers, *Orthosiphon stamineus*, have opened their white flowers with upturned stamens. Some tender grasses have not yet grown as I expected and continue to hope they will. The Blue and Yellow Garden lives up to its name with yellow *Verbesina encelioides*, blue *Salvia farinacea*, and the golden rain tree, *Koelreuteria bipinnata*, in full bloom. Several years ago Jack Shaffer, a friend and gardener in Maryland, warned me of the prolific seeding and ensuing problems of this tree. I responded that thus far I hadn't found a single seedling. He was right. The very next year hundreds of seedlings appeared near and far from the tree. The good news is that they are easy to pull or dig even after several years' growth; the bad news is that there are so many of them.

I plan each day according to the strength of the wells. The one nearest the law office can provide water at low pressure for about an hour, so we let it rest between waterings. The deep well produces the same amount of water per minute, but its deep reservoir holds enough to water all day as long as we don't open the spigot all the way. I go through a mixture of emotions and reactions as I stand for hours holding a hose. Each week I get to every section and study the plants and their response to stress. I always find something coming back into growth. Back-flung petals of *Cyclamen hederifolium* show up against the dark mulch in the woods and pendent white cups of *Leucojum autumnale* brighten the base of the deodara cedar.

Orthosiphon stamineus

Leucojum autumnale

The gardens in urns are lush with colorful solenostemons, chartreuse sweet potatoes (*Ipomoea batatas* 'Margarita'), petunias, phormiums, and other tender plants. The entire garden will look that way with a few soaking rains. Watering is a peaceful occupation despite the heat. Butterflies hover over buddlejas; hummingbirds dash about to their favorite flowers; wasps work on sedums; and bees with bright orange pollen sacks explore *Salvia guaranitica*. If I weren't standing in one place with a hose, I wouldn't take the time to watch them. I pull young weed seedlings accompanied by a bit of music, sometimes a smorgasbord of bits from different pieces, in the back of my mind. The bad aspects of watering are well known, but the good feature—having time to look at every single plant—is often ignored. Old trees, bulbs, and other plants here for seventy years or more console me during this drought and I think each time may be the last time I have to water.

Solenostemon leaves

Late one afternoon the wind grew strong and we heard thunder at a distance. Rain that began at six thirty ended at seven but the lightning and thunder continued. From the kitchen window I saw a bolt of lightning, heard a simultaneous crash of thunder, and saw smoke rising from the woods edge. I knew a tree had been hit, so as soon as I thought it safe I walked down to that area, where I found bits of bark strewn at least fifty feet from our tallest poplar, which had a gash about a foot wide and three or four inches deep from its top to the bottom of the neighboring oak. The lightning had struck the poplar first, then leapt to the oak. I picked up bits of poplar on the ground, but left others thrust too deep into the earth for me to pull out. I felt sick at the thought that we might have to bring heavy equipment into the woods garden to remove the tree. This is a sensitive area filled with *Helleborus niger*. Perhaps the tree won't die and even if it does, we can let it decay and fall slowly the way trees do in the wild. Besides, I have many more little Christmas rose seedlings and can start all over!

Two of our old cats have some of the problems of old age. Both are deaf. They each sit in separate corners of the laundry room and kitchen facing the wall and they yowl, making loud, wailing sounds. When we come to them, they make a normal meow. We believe they have the beginnings of feline Alzheimer's. One of them, Cindy, has taken to her bed and rises only to walk gingerly down the ladder to use the litter box. The other, Impy, continues to go outside. She comes in, eats, and goes out again and again for the first half hour of each day, after which she settles down to sleep in a nest of leaves beneath the old ash tree.

Hillsborough imposed mandatory water restrictions on its customers in July. The mayor and town board requested the state to allow the town to draw more water from the Eno River, the south boundary of our property, and their request was denied. The town depends on the sale of water to help balance its budget, but the life of the river depends on a minimum in-stream flow. In August the town declared this a Stage 5 Water Restriction area. The restrictions are simple: no outdoor water use is permitted, and no water may be wasted. There are signs on many lawns: "Well water used here" or "Non municipal water source used for irrigation." We go to Stage 6 soon unless we get a good rain. We will find out what Stage 6 means if we get there. If it means rationing, I can't think how they will manage it.

Masses of foliage provide the best show in the garden in late summer: solenostemons, durantas, plectranthuses, and purple-bladed grasses. The color of their leaves grows more intense as the days grow shorter. This is high-maintenance gardening. There is almost nothing natural about it. We group these plants together in order to water them easily and they love heat and humidity. The garden would be much more subdued without them, but they are the first plants I would abandon if I didn't have good help or a decent well nearby.

Temperatures went from the nineties to the sixties and we were comfortable again in the garden and nursery. When we returned to the woods, I felt the most exhilarating sense of relief as I fell to my knees, pick in hand, to remove weeds near the colchicums and cyclamen. The white-flowered, fragrant viburnum, *Viburnum farreri* 'Candidissimum', by the old hackberry stump has mostly black leaves, but because the tips of the stems are tinged with crimson, and it has healthy green leaves near the base, I still hope that it will survive. I can live with black leaves as long as I see a sign of life somewhere.

With great excitement and anticipation we repot bulbs every August. We turn over each pot, dump its contents onto a tray, and search through the dirt to see whether the bulbs have multiplied. This is the ultimate treasure hunt! Because I didn't repot them last summer, I was afraid of what I might find. We were most excited to find two corms of *Tecophilaea cyanocrocus* where before there was only one.

Rain brought masses of oxblood lilies, *Rhodophiala advena*, into bloom in the front gardens. The nodding flowers look dark red at first glance, but on closer inspection we saw both dark and light shades on each petal. A subtle streak of lighter red, tinged faintly with yellow, marks the center of each petal, which becomes darker red and finally green at the base. Some creature has already eaten a few flowers and may get them all if I don't protect them in some way. Seeds of clematis planted two years ago, cyclamen, and iris germinated in the dungeon at the end of the month. That's news! Fall approaches.

SEPTEMBER

The month began with rain falling gently for a day and a night. More than four inches fell into the rain gauge, but I wanted more. Leaves on the trees perked up, green grass grew up through brown bases, and fall bulbs pushed up new leaves and flowers. The nodding white, pink, or cerise flowers of *Cyclamen hederifolium* brighten the dark ground beneath the metasequoias while others bloom in the lawn nearby. Craufurd's mowing won't kill them whereas my moving them might, so they remain where we enjoy their leaves all winter. *C. coum* has new leaves and swelling buds full of promise. Cyclamen led me to my life's work. I saw them in England nearly forty years ago and first grew them in Durham where three or four plants dominated my daily garden tour. I searched for signs of life during their summer dormancy, and always paused before them when they were in active growth. After Craufurd and I moved to Hillsborough, I wanted to grow all the available hardy species. That was before I had a greenhouse. After the greenhouse was constructed, I accumulated many forms, and color variants of most known species. In September cyclamen return to growth in the greenhouse; four species bloom in the garden; others produce new leaves; and I feel that same exhilaration and excitement I have come to expect at this season. They grow in and along the road to the pond, in ditches and throughout the woods where they have naturalized, and in the grass around the house. Plants that grow accidentally in the lawn are forgiven, people who plant them there are not.

More oxblood lilies bloom by the path through the Metasequoia Garden, and the young leaves of *Ipheion uniflorum* (spring starflower) are three or four inches high. Rain brought forth more flowers on *Zephyranthes smallii* and *Z. citrina* in the Dianthus Walk. The bed near the boxwoods looks like

Cyclamen hederifolium

I imagine it all year, with masses of colchicum flowers in medium shades of mauve-pink above black mondo grass, *Ophiopogon planiscapus* 'Nigrescens', verbenas, and *Euphorbia dulcis* 'Chameleon'. A few alliums (*A. stellatum*) and more rain lilies (*Zephyranthes* 'Labuffarosea' and *Z. candida*) bloom with them. *Cyclamen graecum* and *Leucojum autumnale* (fall snowflake) are in flower beneath the deodara cedar. Although the cyclamen have larger flowers, broader masses of the white snowflakes show up better at the edge of the circle of brown mulch. Leaves on the fall scilla (*Scilla autumnalis*) are two to three inches high now that the flowers are over. The season has changed. August never brought the fresh crisp air I hoped for but this morning I saw the first leaves of chickweed—a sure sign of fall.

The pond returned to its normal size. Beaches that were nine feet wide vanished beneath the new water. The excess runs over the spillway again and we hear the musical rush of water over our little waterfall. The egret will probably move on now that the marshy edges are under water. This, our largest rainfall in more than a year, brings a sense of release from the stress of the past. Perhaps this drought is over. Weather forecasters see a tropical disturbance in the Atlantic south and east of us, heading our way. I don't want a hurricane, no matter how dry we are. I will leave every little tree and shrub that might be alive until spring reveals the damage from this summer's drought. Perhaps a few plants that look dead will leaf out or sprout from the base. It's official: by the first week in September we had endured over sixty-five days of temperatures at ninety or higher this summer. It wasn't just my imagination.

The soil in the Dianthus Walk is moist at last. Although many plants smothered with grit last winter developed new roots at the surface, they still sprawl, so I divided them and set each rooted bit deeper into soil and gravel. I did the same with every scrap of *Phlox subulata* 'Gingham' and watered

Rain lilies

in each plant with a weak solution of Miracle-Gro. As I worked, I imagined the garden in bloom as I believe it will be next May.

One day I nearly quit at five o'clock, but returned to the woods garden for a final look. I wanted to see whether more colchicums and rain lilies were blooming. When I reached the Mother-in-Law Walk, the sun came out and I saw that slanting light I longed for all August. I felt a burst of new energy and weeded out microstegium until I could no longer see. I found cyclamen in growth and young hellebore seedlings, pulled out *Helleborus foetidus*, and left *H. niger*. How I would love to live without a clock or a calendar! I would wake with the sun and go to bed when I pleased. It would make me more sensitive to all growing things, bird sounds, and insects. Last weekend I heard the owls for the first time in a while. Their song at this season isn't the "Who cooks for you" one we hear in late winter but "Who, who, who, who, who, who cooks." In this house, Craufurd shops and I cook.

The fragrance of vesper irises, *Pardanthopsis dichotoma*, blooming at the back of the house greets me when I come in from the garden. They really aren't irises at all, even though the flowers have standards and falls. A fan of bluish-green leaves appears in early spring and by late summer the flowering stem elongates; its buds swell and open to purple flowers in late afternoon. Each flower lasts only an evening before twisting into a spiral and dropping off, but fresh ones open each day for six weeks or so.

We had our in-house critique tour of the garden today. Every gardener needs a friend—I am lucky to have three—who will walk through the garden and say, "Yes, that is good, let it stay," or "No, that must be removed." After our review and discussion, we cleared the walks and now see the Albert Memorial more clearly. We removed large pink-seeded castor beans. Heavy stalks of the magnificent *Yucca aloifolia* collapsed in the rain-soaked soil, so we sawed and removed the fallen ones and others that grow too near the path and threaten visitors with their stiff, sharply pointed leaves. At the end of the afternoon I returned to the woods, planted new colchicum corms, and weeded until I could do no more. These are the days when I feel my age.

Some aroids are shutting down for winter. When we found leaf stalks of amorphophallus turning yellow and lying on the ground, we brought them in their pots to the greenhouse and set them under a bench where they can remain dry until February or March. As shoots appear on the recently potted bulbs under the benches, we place them on the shelves where they have good light and will bloom all winter.

When I wandered through the garden one evening, I watched a moth dive into the base of datura flowers. The long proboscis must be extraordinarily flexible, for the insect flew into the base of every flower and emerged with proboscis shaking but intact. The moth systematically investigated every newly opened blossom, flying past buzzing flies that look and sound like honeybees and small, black wasps. None of these creatures paid any attention to me as I stood hovering over the flowers, hoping to see what they saw.

By early fall the roses had grown beyond our expectation so I returned to the top of the lath house and tucked in the new long whips. I hadn't lost my nerve. We wove the side pieces into the slats and we did the same for *Rosa* 'Mary Wallace' on the arbor at the entrance to the Tropical Garden. The tasks were pleasant with temperatures and humidity lower than in July.

By mid-month the colchicum garden reached its peak and a haze of pinkish lilac at a distance became hundreds of flowers up close. Flowering *Cyclamen mirabile* joined *C. graecum* under the deodara cedar and masses of *C. hederifolium* bloomed near the metasequoias. Occasionally a cyclamen flower stands out from all the others. Yesterday it was a large white one near the tree. Even though fall is eagerly awaited, I find myself longing for Christmas roses and fall snowdrops. Gardeners are never content.

The rains in late August produced a great flush of new growth in the

Colchicum flowers

sunny gardens and we wait, as patiently as possible, for buds to appear on the late-flowering salvias. Will they bloom on our Garden Open Day in late September? Will the chrysanthemums and asters open? Will the rain lilies continue to bloom? When will we have rain again?

The last bulbs were potted by the middle of the month. This is a remarkable feat, one not accomplished for the past ten years. The staff made it possible. We are congenial. We share the same vision and work toward a common goal—the perfection of the garden. It is, for me, the best of times.

The sight of the first green tips of *Sternbergia lutea* sent me to the woods' edge where I found *S. sicula* var. *graeca* in bloom. This early blooming sternbergia, smaller than its better-known cousin, has clear yellow flowers and pointed petals only about eight inches above ground. This flower is one of the harbingers of fall. Although we will be hot again, the sun won't be higher in the sky for six months or so. Days are noticeably shorter and the pale gray early morning light flattens trees into silhouettes, leaving their tops suffused with light.

I worked to remove the enormous oak stump in the Mother-in-Law Walk. This remnant of a magnificent tree has lain on the north side of the path for six years and I see the mass of red sub-soil in its tangle of roots whenever I approach the woods. Cyclamen, primroses, trilliums, and special hellebores grew in the shade of this tree until the violent winds of Hurricane Fran brought it down. That storm in the fall of 1996 was the worst in my gardening life. Gabrielle McDermit came to work the morning after the storm, arriving at the normal time with barely a gallon of gas in her tank. She worked with Craufurd and me until we could hardly move. Gabrielle will always remain a heroine for us, not only because she came when we were so desperately in need but because she brought fresh, hot coffee the second morning. She first worked at Montrose while studying landscape architecture at North Carolina State University and returned several years

Chrysanthemum

later when her husband practiced medicine in Raleigh. She is tall, beautiful, with long dark hair and a cheerful, pleasant manner. Full of energy, and a superb plants person, she made a great contribution to the garden during her time here. It was a sad day when they moved to Vermont.

That oak fell across my special woodland plants, many from my mother's wildflower garden. Craufurd cut the trunk into small chunks and we made low barrier fences around young big-leaf magnolias, *Magnolia macrophylla*. That worked. The deer could not or would not step on them to reach the small trees. The base of the oak tree still lies where it fell, a reminder of that dreadful storm. I took a mattock, two shovels, a garden fork, and a garden rake to remove it. The soil from the roots fell into the garden and a great cavity remained behind the uprooted tree. I shoveled the earth back into the hole, layering it with compost, weeds, and bits of decayed wood from the stump. Although I didn't eliminate it, I did reduce it and felt quite proud of my accomplishment, until I showed it to Craufurd and he couldn't see any difference. I won't give up until it's gone!

Hellebores are going dormant. The leaves of *H. dumetorum* and *H. multifidus* are weak, flimsy remnants of their winter beauty. As they go down, more flowers and buds on *Cyclamen hederifolium* reappear and *C. coum* has fresh new leaves. Although we last weeded the woods gardens in September a year ago, I am encouraged by the small amount of microstegium and other weeds. Young tree seedlings, our main problem, are easily removed. Even though the extraordinarily dry summer was a factor in this year's sparse growth, we are finally gaining control of the woods. We found new growth on summer dormant aroids, new leaves on hybrid hellebores, and a visible border of that little ophiopogon I planted at the edge of the new Snowdrop Walk last winter. Although still a mere fringe of a border, it defines the path and will in time make a fine edging.

In anticipation of Tropical Depression Hanna, heading toward us, we planted five flats of rohdeas in the woods near where, last February, we planted hellebores. Rohdeas survive drought, deep shade, and hungry animals. I use them to separate different seed strains of hellebores, to hide stumps, to mark corners, and to give a rich, dark green color to the woods floor. We selected seeds from dragon types (those with ridges along the leaves) and from plants with variegated leaves but must wait four or five years for young seedlings to reveal their final form and leaf characteristics. I have never seen one I didn't like.

We worked in the nursery to prepare for Garden Open Day. The sales area has never looked better, with similar plants grouped together and a little space between varieties. We weeded and labeled every pot and divided *Tanacetum parthenium* 'Aureum', the golden-leaved feverfew. It is fun to take a plant that looks bedraggled, pull it apart, cut off the old leaves and tangled remnants of former beauty. When planted deeper in a new pot with fresh soil, it often looks better right away. We worked on the variegated mint, *Mentha suaveolens* 'Variegata'; a golden-leaved oregano, *Origanum vulgare* 'Aureum'; *Helleborus* x *hybridus* and miscellaneous pot-bound plants. Cally lay at our feet, Roger on the potting bench, and Beanie on the stairs.

Craufurd and I handed out a few Garden Open Day notices at the farmers' market and responded to anxious questions, assuring our friends that the garden is fine despite the summer. In fact I am thrilled with the way it looks. The sunny gardens approach their peak. *Helianthus* 'Lemon Queen, blue salvias, and *Caryopteris incana* with whorls of blue flowers bloom in the Blue and Yellow Garden. Red-purple *Lepechinia hastata*, lavender *Salvia leucantha*, and purple-blue *S. mexicana* are open in the Aster Border and ten- to

twelve-foot-high bananas (*Musa basjoo*) enclose the Tropical Garden. After the worst of all summers, perhaps this will be the best of all falls. We are always delighted to look up from our work to see a little black dog and one or more gray tabbies watching us. Colchicums and cyclamen have never been better. We sprayed our deer, woodchuck, and rabbit repellent on all the vulnerable plants, so dahlias are bulking up and beginning to bloom, and I find only a few cyclamen with their flowers bitten off. To make the spray I put one tablespoon of Tabasco sauce, one egg, and a small amount of water into a blender and blend it well. I strain that mixture into a gallon jug, fill the jug with water, and add one tablespoon of dishwashing detergent at the very end. Then I put the mixture into a sprayer and someone sprays everything in the garden we think deer, rabbits, or woodchucks might eat.

We cleaned out the basin for the fountain in the lath house, scooping out green, slimy water with watering cans, tossing it on plants in need, and finally scrubbing the sixty-gallon sorghum pot that holds the water. After cleaning the filter we refilled the pot from the well. The gentle sound of falling water lures many creatures during the night and calms me when I weed nearby.

By mid-September glorious days with low humidity, temperatures in the seventies, and the smells of fall confirm the season. The fruity scent of tea olive, *Osmanthus* x *fortunei*, led me to the back of the Boxwood Border. My plant in Durham, grown from a small rooted cutting from a friend's garden, was too large to transplant to Hillsborough, so it was one of the first plants purchased after we moved here. Clusters of small, white flowers appear amid spiny, dark green leaves. Near the old wall I found a bay myrtle, *Myrica pensylvanica*, dead, another victim of the drought. I discovered the flea-inhibiting qualities of its scented leaves when we lived in Durham. We have always lived with cats, most of which have fleas, so I kept vases filled with myrtle in every room in our former house. Fleas aren't as large a prob-

Momordica charantia

lem here, but I want a bay myrtle on the premises just in case they attack. Fortunately, healthy plants still grow near the woods. *Costus speciosus*, the spiral ginger, grows in a pot in the shady garden near the tea olive. Spirals of leaves with furry undersides as soft as silk appear all along its reed-like stem during summer. Crepey, white flowers at the top of the stem protrude from scarlet, overlapping bracts like those on a pinecone.

The wood splitter assumed its summer role as trellis. *Clematis serratifolia* clambers up the east side with dangling soft yellow, bell-like flowers and shaggy-dog seed clusters. The warty, orange fruits of bitter gourd, *Momordica charantia*, split to reveal scarlet-covered seeds. Barry Yinger, a friend and expert plantsman in Pennsylvania, gave me rectangular, rough, hard beige seeds unlike any I had ever seen. "Plant them in spring after the last frost," he said. "You will like it." I have the greatest respect for Barry so took the seeds, but didn't have the nerve to ask the necessary questions. Should I soak the seeds first? Should I crack them open? I planted them, they germinated, and, he was right, I do like them. Now they germinate on their own after lying all winter at the base of the wood splitter.

The garden smells of fall — wet leaves, mushrooms, and mosses — when we walk slowly through the woods to the pond, looking for cyclamen flowers and leaves and signs of the night creatures. The great blue heron still visits the pond but the little egret left.

We continue to refine the garden. We must remove spent flowers from the buddlejas. We must edge every bed. I must remove the dead stalks from a vicious cactus. We must eliminate oxalis everywhere. We must remove dead branches from shrubs that suffered most in summer's drought. Garden Open Day approaches and several gardens look as we hoped they would. The Blue and Yellow Garden has nearly reached its fall pinnacle. Jo's Bed has never looked better, with a profusion of lespedezas. The gracefully pendulous stalks of *L. thunbergii* 'Gibraltar' have masses of carmine flowers and our own *L. thunbergii* 'White Fountain', a plant found on this property, has pristine white flowers and an elegant weeping form. Two seedling lespedezas, *L. t.* 'Jo's Pink' and *L. t.* 'Pink Fountain', help give the bed its character. The musk rose, *Rosa moschata*, with clusters of white flowers, leans over an arbor, and thornless *R.* 'Bleu Magenta' grows into and over the fence.

When I work on the Rock Garden, I think of my mother's and grandmother's rock gardens. My grandmother in Tennessee (my father's mother) had a cool rock garden filled with native plants growing between limestone rocks at the end of her lawn. It was far enough from the house for me to believe I was invisible when there. She threatened to punish me if I stepped off a rock, but I found it easy to walk through the garden stepping from stone to stone away from my cousins and out of sight of my parents. Mother's rock garden contained special stones, brought to her by her former fourth-grade students and their parents. The land sloped away from the house and we had to go to the bottom of the hill into a grassy dell to see it properly. A low wall at the bottom separated the garden from the grass, and steps on the east and west sides connected it to the garden above. Miniature succulents, small bulbs, and phloxes mingled with the stones in the middle, and a row of *Selaginella braunii*, clubmoss, partly covered the rock wall at the lowest point. My first rock garden was built with stones from my father's property in Chatham County. Craufurd set the stones into the bank and built a retaining wall shortly after we returned from Japan. We had visited many gardens in Kyoto and came away convinced, as was our host, that the stones would tell us how they wish to be placed if we just studied them long enough. The stone work was successful; my garden wasn't.

When we moved here, a mound of green at the west side of the circle of lawn in front of the house covered the remnants of a rock garden. The Grahams told us that it had been made in an earlier period and that their parents hadn't done much with it. I was excited to have full sun for my new garden and neglected the mound for about three years. When I cleared it, I found stones of white quartz with streaks of black lichen. After clearing the honeysuckle and poison ivy off the area, I discovered clumps of bearded iris and masses of ivy and *Vinca minor* (periwinkle), but I was horrified by the bright white stones newly uncovered, and so left a little ivy to soften their glare. Now I know better. There is no such thing as a little ivy. Every year since then I have cut, pulled, and dug out the ivy. I did it again this fall. As for the bright white stones, I like them now. White flowers don't show up against them but everything else does. Recent rains softened the soil and I weeded the entire area, pulling out periwinkle, grasses, and the ubiquitous oxalis. I found cyclamen in leaf or flower, the tips of crocuses about to bloom, and foliage on hoop petticoat narcissuses, *Narcissus bulbocodium*. This is a garden full of illusion. A tiny bulb beside a large stone seems even smaller than it is. The stone becomes a mountain.

The first bus tour of the fall season arrived in the middle of the month. We don't have facilities for buses here, so the driver had to park next to the fence between us and Cameron Park Elementary School. About thirty minutes before they were due, I went down to our entrance, where I weeded the

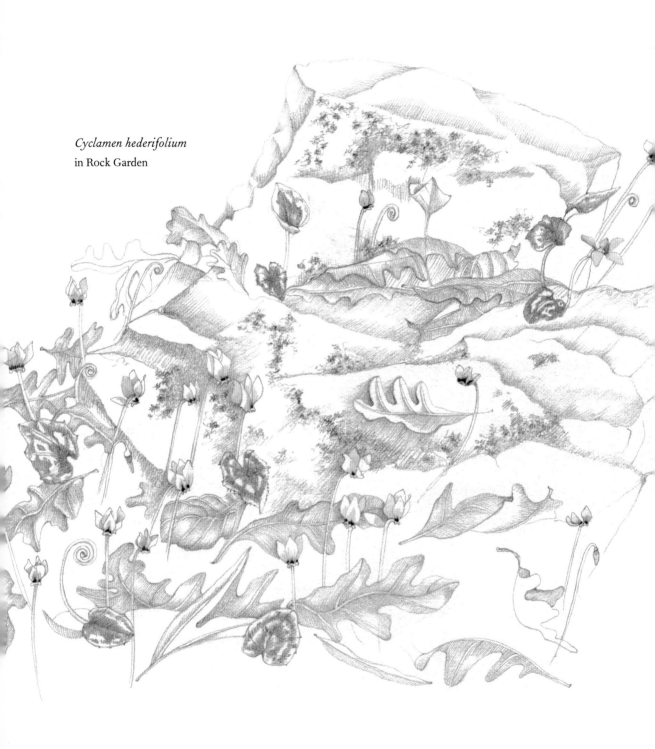

Cyclamen hederifolium
in Rock Garden

edge of the driveway. As their arrival time drew nearer, I felt slight apprehension and exhilaration. Will they think the garden worth coming to see? My fear was based on the weather during this summer. The garden isn't as full as it usually is. The grasses aren't as tall as they should be. Leafless trees remain in hope that a spurt of growth next spring will prove they are alive. The excitement comes from anticipating a garden tour with knowledgeable gardeners. When I heard the roar of the engine as the enormous bus came up the hill past St. Matthew's Episcopal Church, I rushed toward the entrance nearest our fence, waving my arms, to direct the bus into its parking spot as far from the school as possible.

After I gave the group a brief introduction to the staff, and miscellaneous information about the property, including the dates of the house, outbuildings, and how much land we are trying to manage, we walked slowly through the garden. I usually walk backwards, occasionally tripped up by a trusting cat that leads the way and suddenly flops over on his back. I told about each section of the garden, the soil, our reason for its design, and then pointed out individual plants that might otherwise be missed. I tried to refrain from saying how much better it looked last week or may look the following week, but I often mentioned plants not visible and those that will bloom at a different season.

We divided *Sternbergia lutea*. Many clumps are so thick the bulbs lie one on top of the other so the topmost ones cannot get their roots to soil beneath. I dug a bucket full to grow on the east side of the Circle Garden in full sun. Before we could plant them we had to remove the hellebores in distress. After the large white oak died in 1998, hellebores growing there have struggled in the summer sun, so this spring I vowed to move them into cooler shady soil if they survived just one more summer. Although the leaves had disappeared, I found buds below ground about to spring into growth. I dug two hybrids, 'Queen of the Night' brought from Elizabeth Strangman's Washfield Nursery in England, and my only hellebore with dark purple, double flowers, plus a group of *H.* x *ericsmithii*, hybrids recreated here by crossing *H. niger* with *H.* x *sternii*. I divided all of these clumps, and we planted them in the woods along the road to the pond. We watered them with rainwater collected in buckets below the barn roof and mulched them with leaves deposited in the path nearby years ago. The thrill of saving those plants and the vision of them growing in their new environment kept us invigorated. We never complained about walking uphill to fetch water.

Late in the month we spent two days with representatives of the Garden Conservancy. This meeting, arranged in late spring, was one of the primary deadlines toward which we worked all summer. We hoped the garden would look its best. Bill Noble and Marco Stufano arrived early one cloudy, misty morning to look at the garden. They told us that Montrose was unanimously approved as a Preservation Project of the Garden Conservancy, a national, nonprofit organization whose purpose is to help secure the future of designated gardens. Frank Cabot, of New York, was instrumental in establishing the organization and continues to be a leader in spirit and deed. I am thrilled and relieved to think we are closer to ensuring that the work begun here over a hundred and sixty years ago will continue for the foreseeable future. We walked slowly over most of the controlled area and spoke of plants, the basic structure of the garden, the philosophy behind our approach to its development and management, and the history of the place. We walked along the new path to the overlook and they heard of my hope to clear the undergrowth there and incorporate that section into the woodland garden. I showed them the new Snowdrop Walk with its thousands of bulbs invisible below ground. As we walked to the pond, I pointed out my incursions into the edges of the woods where special forms of hellebores and cyclamen grow away from pollinators that might corrupt the strains.

When we had dinner in the evening with Craufurd, we began more serious discussions over the Garden Conservancy's potential role in helping us set in place the necessary legal structure to continue the garden after we can no longer manage it. We haven't worked it out. For one thing, we want to retain absolute control over the direction of the garden as long as possible. I see the Garden Conservancy as an oversight organization to help ensure that our vision is realized.

When Patti McGee, chairman of the garden selection committee, joined us the next day, we discussed the feasibility of our joint effort. We explored the financial requirements and expected expenses and spoke of the further complication of setting up the house as a museum for our collection of Bloomsbury art. There remain many unresolved issues, including determining the correct time to seek tax-exempt status and to set up an advisory board. It is somewhat inhibiting to think of doing anything legally binding when the work of the place proceeds smoothly without it. At the same time we both realize that our condition can change without a moment's notice, and we must prepare for that.

Tropical Depression Isidore brought mist and light rain as it came from Louisiana heading north, west of the Appalachians. We prepared for Garden Open Day. We weeded, made signs, and gathered and labeled cyclamen for sale from the greenhouses. We hope the signs will guide people to the sales area and give them necessary information about some of the plants. Ippy painted them in Bloomsbury style with whorls, dabs, and stylized flowers, and we laminated them so they can withstand rain and wind, and secured them on stakes.

We rolled up the slatted blinds on the greenhouse to let in more light and placed the bulbs now in growth on the glass shelves by the windows. This operation is not as simple as it sounds. In order to roll up a blind I stepped slowly and parted carefully the ginger lilies, *Hedychium coronarium*, near the big greenhouse. I pulled aside the tall green stalks topped with heavenly scented white flowers, grasped the cord, and passed it out to someone. She

Hedychium coronarium

pulled it and rolled the blind over the edge of the angled window, finally handing the cord back to me to fasten to the wall.

We found a few ginger lilies in the garden when we moved here. I didn't know the plant. I had never seen an iris with such large rhizomes and couldn't think what else it could be. To be safe, I dug, potted, and protected several pieces that first winter, in the little glassed-in section of the porch. When they bloomed the following year, I identified them but read that experts consider them hardy only to Zone 9. We live in Zone 7a, so for years I mulched the roots with a foot or two of juniper branches. This mound of needles and branches provided perfect insulation and the plants multiplied until we had so many flowers they perfumed the entire back sunny gardens. After we planted the Tropical Garden, we moved our original plants to the base of the large greenhouse, where they receive the runoff from the roof.

We built our first greenhouse when I began the nursery in 1984. I had grown cyclamen and boxwoods for several years in preparation for my nursery and ordered a Lord and Burnham greenhouse that I believed would be large enough for everything I might ever want to grow. Before the construction was finished, I had run out of room, so we built a second bench and put it on top of the central one in the middle of the building. We put two rows of shelves on the wall of our house and three on the exterior wall of the greenhouse. Although the extra space helped, in less than two years I ordered a free-standing structure about four times the size of the original one. When I filled that, I stopped. By then I had discovered that most plants I want to protect grow best in a cold environment. We built deep cold frames to winter over my hardiest "tender" perennials. Really hardy plants for sale survived the winter in pots set in shredded bark mulch without further protection until late spring, when threatened frosts often forced us to cover those in growth with reemay, a light-weight, nonwoven fabric.

Little showers off and on during the morning didn't deter us from preparing for Garden Open Day. We had planned to weed eat the edges of buildings and walls while Craufurd mowed, but the weed eater wouldn't start, so we crawled around the base of every structure with clippers, rakes, and baskets and removed the wispy growth of neighboring weeds and grasses. Then, wearing knee pads and with linoleum cutters in hand, we weeded the crevices between the bricks on the patio outside the back door. With whisk brooms and dustpans we collected the dirt and weeds as we went along. We were so proud of how it looked, we made Walter McClements look at it. Walter was here to remove the year-old hornets' nest from the side of the house and preserve and reset the covers on the deep cold frames. Finally we scrubbed and refilled the birdbaths and sprayed our pepper concoction on all the choice plants that might be eaten by deer and woodchucks during the night.

Garden Open Day was cool and cloudy and the staff was here by seven thirty. We set out chairs and pounded in the stakes bearing signs telling people not to go into the woods, the lath house, and other forbidden places. Craufurd set up his table with a sign-up sheet for the mailing list, a few of Allen Lacy's and my books for sale, and some academic work to do during slow periods. We put out the plant signs and filled a large cooler with lemonade. Marsha Ferree, friend and official bean counter, came wearing a blue dress and large straw hat to stand at the top of the driveway, greet people, hand out brochures, and count the visitors. Helga MacAller helped with sales. We first met Helga at her stand at the Hillsborough farmers' market. She is slim, of Danish origin, with dark hair and a ready laugh, sparkling eyes, and energy to spare. Most important, she introduced me to Cathy, who first came to Montrose for Helga's birthday celebration. Although we were ready by ten, our first visitors had been in the garden since nine thirty.

The day was wonderful—never hot. The garden was better groomed than ever and, although some plants didn't perform as well as they would with summer rains, others bloomed better than ever. We caught no one trying to slip into the woods, step into the beds, or steal plants. After everyone left, we sat under the oak tree and told of our experiences, all of which were good. Cally met everyone who visited the nursery. She went up the hill to greet them and, with tail wagging, led them to the sales area. Roger spent the morning on the roof of the potting room — a new experience for all of us. He cried plaintively but when I climbed up to the edge of the roof, he wouldn't come near me. Shortly after lunch I watched him walk down the exterior of the chimney where the bricks are laid in stair-like steps. When he reached the lowest one, he fell into the fig bushes. He wandered with some visitors through the garden and finally settled near us at the edge of the parking lot. After everyone left, he leapt with joy, pranced sideways, and ran in circles. The other cats remained in hiding. Beanie spent his day on the lath house ledge, where he believed he was invisible.

This was an extraordinary week for the garden at Montrose.

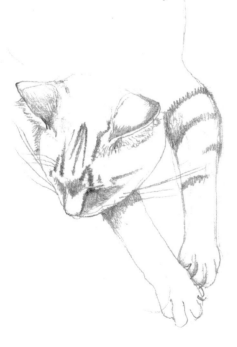

OCTOBER

I sold my piano to our neighbor, Michael Malone. I hadn't played it for years, don't want to live with it as just a piece of furniture, and he is eager to play it. As soon as he told me the movers would arrive the next day, I wanted to go away. I thought I couldn't face seeing it leave the house. When the movers walked with my instrument out the dining room door, I stood back and watched while they loaded and secured it in the van. I was amazed. It wasn't sad at all. This was a symbol of part of my life that ended years ago. I still have the harpsichord. I have an instrument to play if I reach the stage when I can garden no longer. And if we just have a few more cold, wet days in winter, I will not have to wait until I am too feeble to get around. I will learn the Goldberg Variations.

Early October was hot and humid. Frost will lay the garden in a heap upon itself before long and I cannot let the heat lure me into complacency or let discomfort drive me inside. During the first week of October we set the hardiest plants in pots in the shallow cold frames. These are the survivors, the ones that can stand frozen roots. The next hardiest plants went into cold frames two to three feet below ground, where even in our coldest winter, temperatures do not drop below twenty-eight degrees. Plants that must not freeze but can withstand cold air down to thirty-eight degrees went into the greenhouses. A few cordylines, ferns, and phormiums went into the pit below the law office, and tender tropicals went into the warm basement to join solenostemons under fluorescent lights on a couple of plant stands.

After dealing with about a tenth of the plants in the nursery, I wondered whether I have nine days left before frost? During the next week we brought in tender salvias, took cuttings of special plectranthuses and solenostemons, and dug echeverias from urns and from the ground. Each day began anxiously and ended with a greater sense of security. Worry coupled with the fear of an unknown frost date kept me on edge. I have tours to give and haven't finished removing the microstegium in the woods garden. I mustn't let this weedy grass go to seed again.

Buds and flowers mixed with new, dark green leaves clothe *Clematis cirrhosa* on the large *Juniperus virginiana* at the entrance to the Metasequoia Garden. Silvery-gray foliage on the starflowers, *Ipheion uniflorum*, covers the ground south of the metasequoias, and more leaves on *Cyclamen hederifolium* signal an end to their flowering. The days are cooler now so jeans and sweatshirts have replaced summer's shorts and sleeveless shirts. Soon the heaters in the potting room and greenhouse will be cleaned in preparation for winter. Each day brings us one step closer to that inevitable killing frost, so we bring in more and more tender plants. By the end of the first week in October last year we had had our first frost and several years before that we received that deathly blow on September 25. Our race is against time.

I led a group of friends, as I do most visitors, by the bank and then into the shade of the metasequoias where we paused before cyclamen in flower or leaf. It was all I could do to keep from getting on hands and knees to weed chickweed, *Stellaria media*, and henbit, *Lamium amplexicaule*, that grow lustily amid all the choice winter plants. Both weeds are easy to remove, and that would improve the bed instantly. The dramatically marked leaves of *Arum italicum* reminded me to look for a flower on *A. pictum* and I found its single, dark velvety-purple flower fully open beneath the metasequoia. We stepped carefully into the bed to examine the flower closer but its foul odor drove us away quickly. Perhaps, this year, gnats or flies will smell it, too, and I will get fertile seeds.

I live in the future now, longing for the first snowdrop before fall crocuses have reached their peak, but I must discipline myself and continue taking the garden and nursery apart to protect those tender plants I may never find again. What I long to do is plant, weed, and extend the paths along the woodland terraces.

Rain for two days left 6.3 inches in our gauge — a new record. Even though we put bags of shredded leaves on both sides of the west door of the greenhouse, several inches of water quickly covered the floor. I wished for sandbags. As I dug each tender plant for the staff to pot up, water quickly filled its hole. I went through two pairs of jeans, two pairs of socks, one pair of "waterproof" pants, a raincoat with a tear in the wrong place, and a pair of waterproof shoes before I found clothes that kept me dry. The Eno River became a broad swirling mass flooding the land below the gardens and dam. The pond, though brown, looked calm, but water flowed rapidly through the spillway, roaring as it fell over rocks on the way to the river.

Rainwater soaked into the gravel of the greenhouse during the night and I removed the bags of leaves the next day. My afternoon was spent planting seedling irises, the only surviving cardoon (*Cynara cardunculus*), and golden feverfew (*Tanacetum parthenium* 'Aureum') into the Circle Garden and tiny dianthuses and alliums in the scree. The ground was moist as deep as I could dig. If we get the forecast rain, the plants will take root quickly.

I hear geese coming to and from the pond each morning and evening. I would know it is fall without a calendar. In fact, I believe I would know without stepping out of the house. Hackberry leaves litter the laundry room floor by the end of each day. In summer, grass clippings end up there and up the back stairs, while in winter and spring a light coating of mud sometimes sprinkled with sawdust confirms the season.

We race the squirrels for the pecans. I hope it will be a good year — the first since 1997. Two trees west of the house have clusters of nuts at the tips of their branches. Crows and blue jays scream at each other during the day and raccoons and deer come at night and leave the water in the birdbath muddy, littered with pecan hulls and bits of nuts. Several times a day I walk around and around each tree in a carefully planned way to search for pecans in every square foot of a thirty-foot radius.

Chinese lantern-like seedpods decorate the golden rain tree, *Koelreuteria bipinnata*, in the Blue and Yellow Garden. We see that tree, the tallest one in the summer gardens, from every corner of the sunny gardens. We made the Blue and Yellow Garden in the early 1990s in the lowest area of the old kitchen garden where formerly we grew corn and melons. Banks covered with Bermuda grass surrounded the bed on two sides. I had begun to invade the area shortly after moving here, planting daylilies and kniphofias on the east side and an assortment of perennials on the north. Gradually the narrow strips of ornamentals became broader and the area for vegetables narrower. After we gave up vegetable gardening, Craufurd planted crimson clover for winter, alternating with buckwheat in summer. We cringed when visitors said his field of clover was the prettiest part of the garden. Craufurd replaced the grassy banks with retaining walls built of stone picked up on the property and we settled on a cool blue and yellow color scheme for this, the hottest part of the garden. I had experimented with these colors in a little strip next to the Aster Border where I grew flax (*Linum perenne*), anthemis, and Chinese delphiniums (*Delphinium grandiflorum*).

When Mother was in the hospital with her final illness, she gave me the little iron gate leading to property near their Durham home. She said I would find the fence that went with it in the basement of their house. I knew the gate well, but had never seen the fence. Paul Gove, Hillsborough's talented blacksmith, repaired the fence, surveyed the site, and told us exactly how and where to put the wall. We wanted it in roughly the same place where there had been a cedar post-and-wire fence. Smitty, a superb stonemason from Chapel Hill, built the stone wall beneath the fence, Wayne constructed steps leading from this level to the rest of the garden, and we planted a circle of young boxwoods rooted from those near the house. We needed an object for the central axis of the paths that intersect the main path. We wanted something to slow our passage through the garden. A millstone from my

parents' garden was too low, a large copper vessel too small, but finally we found a sixty-gallon sorghum pot that was just right. Orostachys species grow there in gravelly soil. Buddlejas and vitexes provide yellow or blue flowers in summer. Slow-growing conifers, with needles tinted yellow or blue, surround the garden, making the Blue and Yellow Garden the only one that retains its color all year.

Roger Haile, a friend and artist in Mebane, photographed this garden throughout the year. He captured many of the small combinations that make up the bed but, more important, he put this garden into its place within the larger garden. His pictures include the sky, revealing its importance as a blue element in the color scheme, and the area beyond the fence, with the barn and trees in the distance. He made it impossible to forget this year!

We redid the sunny gardens in 1998, lengthening the views by creating longer paths interrupted by urns or plants spilling over the edges of the borders. When we look through the Blue and Yellow Garden now, we see the field beyond the Aster Border and the top of the juniper hedge that separates our land from Cameron Park Elementary School, our neighbor to the west. The sounds of bells and children playing on the school grounds punctuate our days.

When I walk beyond the fence and look back into the gardens, I see the larger picture. Details can't clutter my vision. I become a visitor, no longer the creator and manager, and see it with fresh eyes. Billowing masses of asters and chrysanthemums in flower or bud form arcs of color. Large shrubs and grasses add height and contrast in form. The glory of autumn confirms the work of spring and summer. Each day is important because we have only a few weeks at most before frost alters everything.

That doesn't mean we sit around on the benches contemplating the meaning of life. We work against time. Frost may come tonight or tomorrow. We dig plants, take more cuttings of tender things, fill both greenhouses, the pit below the law office, and the cold frames. We will reorganize the greenhouse benches after every tender plant is protected and arrange the pots so that we can see each plant. Some of this process is automatic, because I remember what happened in past years — what died in the big greenhouse but lived in the smaller one, which plectranthuses are too tender for cold greenhouses. I wish I could remember everything about every year we have done this. When possible, we divide our new, tender plants and test them in several locations. I have no reference book to help with these decisions, but the staff, all younger than I, often remember what I have forgotten.

I look for snowdrops although it isn't cold yet. Mid-October is time for *Galanthus reginae-olgae* to bloom. I didn't find flowers in the Rock Garden, but at the end of the day looked again in the Old Garden at the wood's edge, where I found a bud. Frantically I pulled away chickweed and henbit to uncover other snowdrops in flower or pushing above ground. At last I can look forward to a snowdrop somewhere from now until late March.

We heard the first white-throated sparrows last weekend. At first they sound a little shy, but as the cold weather settles in their song grows stronger and even more attractive. It will sound especially sad to me just before they fly north in May, when I begin to look forward to this day the following fall.

Tony Bradshaw came from London for a weekend visit. He brought more Bloomsbury art. One piece, an early one by Vanessa Bell, is a painting of two stylized women, each holding a fish she is about to drop into a pot. Another, a sketch of men loading boats done by Duncan Grant in pastel shades of yellow, green, blue, red, and purple, is a study for a larger painting in the chapel at Lincoln Cathedral. The third piece is Dora Carrington's tinsel picture of the "Side-Saddle Flower," painted and appliqued on glass. I had never heard of a side-saddle flower when we were offered this picture, but happened to be reading *Ladies' Southern Florist* by Mary C. Rion (a facsimile of the 1860 edition) when we purchased it. She refers to a plant of that name without its botanical name. Thanks to *Hortus Third* I know now that the plant illustrated is *Sarracenia purpurea*.

We came to our interest in Bloomsbury through my parents. My father, Charles Richard Sanders, studied the work of Lytton Strachey and the Strachey family in the 1940s. I remember my parents sending boxes of chocolate and other supplies to members of the Strachey family during the Second World War. He visited them in 1946 and became a friend of Duncan Grant. He knew Lady Strachey and her children: Pippa, Marjorie, James and his wife Alix, and Dorothy and her husband, Simon Bussy. He was also a good friend of Frances and Ralph Partridge, and stayed at Hamspray House several times before Frances moved to London. My parents purchased several paintings by Duncan Grant during those years. When Craufurd and I first met, he and my father spent much time discussing Maynard Keynes, and I was happy to have found a prospective husband who shared an intellectual interest with him. When we lived in Durham, we purchased our first Bloomsbury paintings, a view of Charleston farmhouse painted by Vanessa Bell and portraits of John Maynard Keynes and his wife, Lydia Lopokova, by Duncan Grant. When my mother died in 1992, we brought their collection of about thirteen items to Montrose. Craufurd went to London that summer wondering whether he might add to it, and all roads led to The Bloomsbury Workshop and Tony Bradshaw. On the first trip he purchased a drawing by Roger Fry. After talking with Tony over the phone, he warmly invited him to come to stay with us. He invited a complete stranger whom neither of us had even seen! About a year later Craufurd brought from the airport an attractive man with curly, gray hair, expressive eyes, and a delightful sense of humor and we liked him right away. This was the beginning of our extensive collection of Bloomsbury paintings, drawings, ceramics, porcelain, books, furniture, and fabrics. We never could have done it without Tony.

The three of us went to Ippy's exhibition of drawings at the National

Humanities Center. The Center has excellent space for such a show. Large walls of white-painted brick don't interfere with the art and the daylight coming from many different angles illuminates each piece. The interior reminds me of a ship with a railing and walkways near each item so we can see them up close, but with enormous spaces across which to view them at a distance. The place was perfect for Ippy's art. She showed charcoal drawings of large nudes and flowers with bold outlines. She had compositions of intricate, delicately drawn beasts and imaginary objects inspired by nature, and she displayed one of her major works, *Escape From Eden*, in a beautiful wooden case made expressly for it. We were overwhelmed by the power and beauty of her work in that setting.

By late October fall crocuses bloomed throughout the gardens in the front—the Rock Garden, Metasequoia Garden, and beneath the deodara cedar. *C. tournefortii*, a favorite, has wide cups that never close from the time the first bloom opens until the flower collapses several days later. Thanks to good seed set and germination, new plants appear in unexpected places. Delicate aquilegia-like leaves of *Isopyrum biternatum* cover the top of the mound on which the dawn redwoods grow. The new year has begun. By early January, when humans face a new calendar, this garden will be well into its year.

We long for a little pig—any sort of pig will do. Green acorns littered the ground near the Rock Garden in early September and ripe ones continue to fall from the oaks near the front gardens and scree. Many have germinated and some already have roots four inches long. We must pick up every one before the taproot grows into the ground. Recent rains mean we can pull out the seed and its root with thumb and forefinger tightly pressed. We all worked on the Rock Garden, the surrounding gardens and paths, and hauled away four large carts filled with acorns, but realize we have barely begun. I wish acorns tasted like pecans.

We spent the entire day on the Old Garden, an area between the woods and main sunny gardens, immediately south of the Aster Border. When Craufurd and I first visited Montrose, the Grahams told us the family called it the Old Garden. I was curious. I saw mature bowdocks (*Maclura pomifera*), buckeyes (*Aesculus flava*), an enormous dead juniper with a smooth trunk bleached after years of sunlight, Japanese honeysuckle, and multiflora roses. Large gray stones, some covered with lichen or moss, formed humps throughout the area. Where was the garden, and what grew there? I still don't know what was there before we came, but now it contains our largest collection of snowdrops and is a test area for new seed-grown bulbs and corms. My best *Helleborus multifidus* subsp. *hercegovinus* and *H. vesicarius* grow there along with special forms of *Iris unguicularis*.

We weeded and mulched the area with help from four-legged Roger (two-legged Roger is the photographer), who, as usual, digs when and where we dig. He puts a great deal of energy into it, throwing up the dirt then running while looking back to be certain we see him. Cally lay in the mulch shivering, so we took her to the heater in the potting room. We counted thirty-four *Galanthus reginae-olgae* in bud or flower, and admired the new leaves of *Cyclamen coum*. These plants, some of the best and rarest forms, were grown from wild-collected seeds distributed years ago by the Cyclamen Society. Although I saw a few buds, it will be at least a month before they open.

The changing seasons bring parts of the garden into and out of focus. Although color still fills the sunny gardens, the shady gardens are increasingly more interesting with newly emerging flower buds and leaves. Cyclamen leaves form a ground cover near the large rocks in the woods, and fresh young leaves of many arum species expand daily.

Ippy wanted seeds to draw. We gathered them from silver bells (*Halesia diptera*, and *H. carolina*), *Styrax americanus*, *Koelreuteria bipinnata*, and *Fir-*

miana simplex (Chinese parasol tree). The last was the most interesting, with an oblong, boat-like beige cup and round brown seeds at the edges, perched like passengers in the boat. Most of these little boats had two seeds but some had four or more. I can never resist planting seeds of a few trees. Cheryl, our primary seed sower, does the necessary research to find which treatment will give the best results. When she sows the seeds, she notes in the calendar when to put the flats in cold or warm locations. She has extraordinary success.

Richard Hartlage came to visit. When Bill Hunt first brought him to see the fall bulbs nearly twenty years ago, Richard, a tall, handsome young horticulture student at the University of North Carolina in Raleigh, walked briskly through the garden and responded to plants enthusiastically. When several years later he drove over to show me his shiny new red truck, I secretly hoped he was coming to ask for a job. He was and I eagerly hired him. Richard worked here in the early days of Montrose Nursery, dividing and potting on plants in the little smokehouse, and planning and planting the garden. Richard was delightful to have around. A keen plantsman with a lovely sense of humor, he was eager to learn new plants. As we walked through each section of the garden on this visit, I remembered things he did—his planting our first seedling *Arisaema sikokianum* and our first group of *Iris unguicularis*.

Perhaps the drought is over. Significant rains fell this month and we expect more during the next few days. The pots at the eaves of the buildings overflow and the ground is so fully saturated that we no longer need captured rainwater. The rain fell continuously, so I dashed in and out of the potting room bringing freshly dug hellebores, primulas, salvias, and plectranthus for the staff to divide and pot up. The others worked inside and talked and laughed a lot! I wore lined jeans, a shirt, a fleece shirt, a down vest, heavy socks, and waterproof shoes. Over most of this I had a large pair of water-

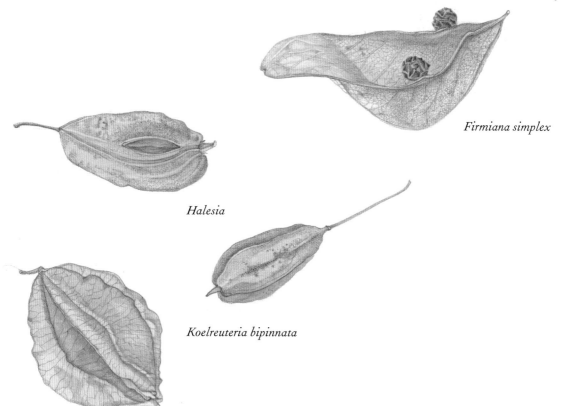

Firmiana simplex

Halesia

Koelreuteria bipinnata

proof overalls with the cuffs rolled up so they caught the rain that ran off my slicker. I was neither cold nor wet. After the rain stopped, we planted phloxes, sanguisorbas, and rohdeas in beautifully moist soil in several places in the garden. It has been five years since the dirt felt like that. More than ten inches of rain fell this month, making it our fourth wettest month since records were kept. The soil is moist and the area outside the potting room so muddy we spread gravel over it. The ground feels more like March than October.

The late fall this year enabled us to enjoy our tender

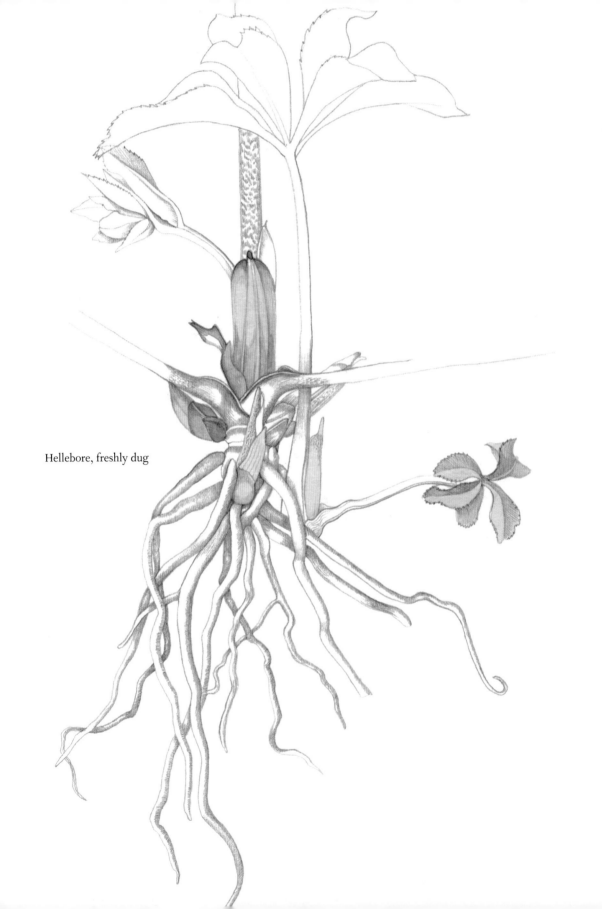

Hellebore, freshly dug

plants in the big urns for four extra weeks. Using a hand saw and standing on a ladder, I cut a circle around the base of each plant and lifted it gently while cutting away the grasping roots at the bottom of the container. This worked and I saved large alpinias, homalocladiums, solanums, and lantanas. I felt a little sad as I destroyed the plantings in the major urns. But whenever I feel like that, I go to another section of the garden to see emerging crocuses or hellebores with fresh leaves. This time I counted galanthuses — fifty-four in bloom or bud. How can I long for the past when a future full of promise is upon me?

Frost and freezing temperatures forecast for the last weekend of the month led us back through the garden to search for forgotten plants. We found salvias, forms of plectranthus, saccharums, and a large phormium. We collected ripe seeds as we went, and whenever we came near

Alpinia zerumbet 'Variegata'

the house, picked up fallen nuts around the pecan trees. We potted the plants, a cartload at a time, and can barely find a spot for a flat in the greenhouse. Cally and Roger stayed with us for most of the day, occasionally chasing each other while we carried over fifteen lexan covers for the cold frames and put away the new hoses inside the former ladies' room in the old outhouse behind the smokehouse. We are ready for winter.

NOVEMBER

Plants, wilted like scalded spinach, make the garden smell like scorched, decaying matter. Charcoal gray, brown, and black replace green, burgundy, and chartreuse. Frost early on the first morning of November and again the next night turned plants into mushy heaps. The shredded leaves of bananas collapsed, broken in the middle. Fat buds on *Dahlia imperialis*, the tree dahlia, blackened; they were showing color in late October. Perhaps they will bloom next year. Frost declared an end to summer. Though painful, fall's first frost is easier to bear than spring's last one. Because it arrived late this year, we brought in tender plants and cuttings at a leisurely pace, returning again and again to search for those we had forgotten or overlooked.

At last we have time to revise the walk below the Blue and Yellow Garden where *Salvia uliginosa* nearly smothered the roses. We dug out much of this salvia and took the long route to the brush pile in order to pass by blooming snowdrops. If I seem a little obsessed by them at this season, it is because I finally found a location where they grow well. The first ones found here grew in the shrub border west of the boxwoods. I added new ones beneath the deodara cedar where they persisted but barely increased and others near the machine shelter where they prospered but were hidden by vigorous grasses. Bulbs in the Rock Garden quickly grew into clumps so thick they barely bloomed and I moved some of them into the Old Garden a year ago. Others remain in the Rock Garden, where visitors can see them and where I know they will continue to multiply. The majority grow in drifts near the gray stones in the Old Garden, an area now named the Snowdrop Woods. I finally found the perfect place, shaded but not bone dry in summer and sunny in winter. My grandmother said there was no better accomplishment than to learn every inch of a piece of property. It takes years to discover places that are moist in times of drought and dry after heavy rains but slowly each place reveals its character.

We went to Ippy's for lunch. We worked on the gardens until shortly before noon, then washed our hands and knees. The day that began with rain turned sunny with the autumn's clear blue sky. Ippy's home, just fifteen minutes away, could be on another planet, or, at the very least, in another country. We drove into the driveway and saw her husband Neil's neatly stacked logs and twigs all exactly the same length, arranged in groups by diameter. Although we were tempted to go into the garden first, manners dictated that we announce our arrival to our hostess. We wandered through the house, admired Roger Haile's new blue and yellow painting that transformed the sitting room into a gallery. The house fits harmoniously into the landscape. Each window frames a view of the pond, a tree, or a bit of sky. We helped carry wine and food for lunch to a table beneath an arbor supporting *Rosa banksiae*. We walked through the garden, admired her aunt's sculpture and the curved brick wall that separates this private space from the road. Special trees were perfectly pruned in her small but exquisitely designed and controlled garden. A 'Mermaid' rose, espaliered against the wall, retained yellow buds and flowers untouched by recent frosts, and both white- and cerise-flowered rugosa roses bloomed in the curving border. Slender, upright conifers grow beside a window in the wall and curved, fragrant, silver-foliaged plants flourish in raised beds supported by brick walls along the walk to the studio.

The pair of Katsura trees, *Cercidiphyllum japonicum*, that flank the entrance to Ippy's studio, smelled faintly of caramel. A round window opposite the front door framed the brilliant leaves and rough gray bark of the trees beyond. We saw a few of her drawings and pictures of her son and daughter on the tables on either side of the room. After the splendid lunch we returned refreshed, eager to continue editing the garden at Montrose.

Now at last we have time to correct the mistakes of the past year. We gave the new Aster Border a haircut. I rescued plants threatened by their neighbors and thinned or removed chrysanthemums, salvias, and asters that were about to smother the roses. Plants that crowded or shaded the reblooming irises went onto the compost pile and daturas that had grown too large and sprawling went onto the brush pile. It is a major gardening challenge to maintain the proper space between plants.

Our first Aster Border was directly south of the lath house in a large square of land formerly filled with rows of asparagus, strawberries, and raspberries. I spent several years pulling out asters and weeds that crowded the berries. Every spring we ate asparagus from the strip along the edge, and one year, and only one year, we had more raspberries than we could eat. Gradually, I planted the boundaries, putting named asters at one end and a collection of blue and yellow flowering plants at the other. I gave up on the raspberries. The new asters prospered and we finally dug out the asparagus.

We placed a large Regency urn, "the big urn," on a brick foundation in the center of the garden and named the entire square the Aster Border. The garden didn't age well. The shrubs quickly grew so large they hid the urn in summer. We transplanted the blue and yellow flowering plants into the new Blue and Yellow Garden and in the late 1990s I removed the asters and divided the large square into four separate beds with wide paths leading to the urn from all four sides. These became the Color Gardens.

Our current Aster Border is the south end of the large strip of land we called, and I still call, the vegetable garden. This, the final portion of the former kitchen garden to change functions, was where we kept plants for sale in pots set in mulch during the nursery years. Blue-purple, pink, or white asters grow there now with white, yellow, or pink chrysanthemums, late-blooming salvias, a few roses, buddlejas, and callicarpas. Verbenas and tradescantias spill into the paths and tender burgundy-leaved grasses (pennisetums and saccharum) become large masses by fall. Large hydrangeas (*H. paniculata* 'Tardiva' and 'Unique'), willows (*Salix alba* var. *sericea*, and *S. purpurea* 'Nana'), and a young *Magnolia ashei*, now a subspecies of *M. macrophylla*, form the background of the planting in summer and provide structure in winter. This garden usually peaks in October just before frost.

Moist soil, mild temperatures, and the promise of more rain led us to major planting projects. We removed the crimson barberries behind the law office, roots and all. These prickly shrubs were planted here because my original plan failed. I had wanted a yew hedge to form the background for the urn that holds *Agave americana*. Yews don't grow easily in this climate so the plant on this property was a special feature, mentioned in articles on the Grahams' garden. I had rooted cuttings from the large yew at the south end of the driveway shortly after we moved here and set my young plants at the edge of a path beside the Cranford Road Bed where they grew well until I found a place for my hedge.

We placed an urn with art deco heads and curving handles on a low brick foundation south of the law office as the focal point looking north from the new gardens. The background was to be a dark green, semi-circular yew hedge, carefully pruned so the view from the law office window wouldn't be lost. All but one yew died when we transplanted them so we substituted burgundy-leaved, seedling barberries, *Berberis thunbergii* f. *atropurpurea*. Their dark leaves were pretty in summer and bright red berries remained well into winter, but there were many months when the leafless plants didn't provide the background I wanted. Besides, barberries are unfriendly to weeders. For the second time we planted a semi-circle of young yews with the hope that my original vision will eventually be realized. It looks a little ridiculous now but I can imagine how it will look in time.

Art deco urn with *Agave americana*

We want a similar thing around the Color Gardens. The plan, stimulated by an idea of Gabrielle's, is to have a hedge of dark green upright boxwoods separating these borders from the rest of the sunny gardens. They would provide a green background to the Blue and Yellow Garden, and enclosure to the square surrounding the big urn. Several years ago I planted over two hundred three-year-old boxwoods, *Buxus sempervirens* 'Pyramidalis', rooted from the one near the big greenhouse. As I watched with despair, the majority died from a soil-borne fungus within a year. Again this fall I planted young, vigorous plants, still hoping for a hedge in a dozen or more years. We stuck more cuttings in case we fail. Patience and time are essential requirements for those who would make a garden. A garden doesn't need to develop as we envision it within a year or even ten years; but we must believe it will happen eventually.

Dark chocolate-colored compost covers the four

Color Gardens. We carried rich brown humus in wheelbarrows up the hill to each bed as we cleared away the old growth. We put the compost on top of last year's leaf mulch and will top that with a fresh layer of new leaves, making a sandwich of leaves filled with compost. Our compost contains spent potting soil saved from repotting plants and urns, refuse from the garden (weeds without seeds and soft prunings), plus meatless scraps from the kitchen. In November, when the weather cools off, we begin each day wearing hats, coats, and gloves and end in shirtsleeves. One day I came up the hill and found the staff lying on the gravel. Cally was sniffing them while Roger pranced about nearby. Upon discovering that no one was injured, I joined them and we lay in the sun looking up at the sky. No one spoke. It was bliss.

After we emptied two compost piles, Craufurd rebuilt one to fill as we clear off the garden. He cut juniper logs twelve feet long and carried them to the compost area north of the woods garden, where he built a square structure, rather like a log cabin, to hold our raw matter. We have two sets of three piles at varying stages of decomposition. We fill the two outer bins of each set, leaving the one in the middle empty. After a year we shovel the piles on either side into the one in the middle, alternating partly decayed compost with leaves from the town. A year later dark brown humus, more valuable than gold, is ready for us to spread onto the garden.

During the days that followed we spread more compost over gardens adjacent to the path south of the Blue and Yellow Garden. We weeded as we went and Cally and Roger played while we worked. Roger chased each plant we tried to remove. He climbed the golden rain tree when we pruned it, and did head bumps with Cally while waiting for us to return with loads of black humus. Freezing temperatures meant we quit early to cover the cold frames before they lost the day's heat.

A tornado watch for central North Carolina brought fear. We lowered

Metasequoia glyptostroboides

the slatted shades on the greenhouses, tied down with bungee cords the lexan covers for the shallow cold frames, and placed bags of shredded leaves on either side of the west door of the big greenhouse to keep out the rain. Because it was Veterans' Day we would hear no warning from the school. Dressed in all my waterproof clothes I dug arums and hellebores, which we potted up. We were lucky. Rain came without damaging wind.

I know more than I want to about tornadoes. The one that touched down in Hillsborough during the years I had the nursery destroyed miles of homes and trees in a few minutes. Two years ago a tornadic downdraft hit us. Martha Blake-Adams, a dear friend who helped pack plants and illustrated the nursery catalog and my book with Allen Lacy, warned me of a tornado heading for Hillsborough, just in time for me to alert everyone working here. Emily Eidenier, a high school intern, was weeding the Dianthus Walk and heard the warning over the loudspeaker at school next door but didn't take it seriously. She later told me they sounded too calm to be serious. Another employee continued digging potting soil. By the time she came in, I was too frightened to leave the greenhouse. Wayne used to park near the barn, where his dog lay waiting for pats and food. When he heard my call, he gathered up the dog and drove his truck to the parking lot seconds before our largest, oldest white oak fell right where his truck and dog had been. If the tree hadn't broken ten feet above ground, it would have destroyed the old barn and its contents.

In the middle of the month I removed masses of *Verbena tenuisecta* from the Dianthus Walk. They smothered their neighbors in their attempt to turn the entire bed into a verbena walk. The ground was warm and I plunged more long strands of dianthus and phlox deeper into the gravelly soil and imagined how it will look at its peak of bloom in May or when frosted with silver in winter. I walk down the brick path that separates the two borders of dianthus every morning and always see something of interest — at least a flower or two and mounds of fragrant gray, purple, or green foliage.

Mahonia x *wagneri* 'King's Ransom'

The fall leaves are the most beautiful ever. At the south end of the field across from our entrance on St. Marys Road, gold, yellow, and orange maple leaves and dark tree branches are vivid against gray sky. Yellowish brown leaves remain on the deciduous magnolias at the edge of the field while *Magnolia macrophylla*, nearer the house, has dropped a blanket of leaves, beige on one side and gray on the other, over the arums and hellebores beneath it. Two white oaks at the crest of the hill retain remnants of green amid their burgundy-brown leaves. Butterscotch needles cling to the metasequoias like draped veils. Leaves on the hardy orange, *Poncirus trifoliata* 'Flying Dragon', turn from orange with yellow and touches of green to pure yellow before falling. Brilliant red leaves of *Nyssa sylvatica*, black gum, that grows where the old cucumber magnolia stood, drop each day, but the dogwoods retain their plum- or currant-colored leaves. The elms at the edge of the driveway are bright yellow and their damp trunks nearly black. The foliage on *Mahonia* x *wagneri* 'King's Ransom' slowly changes from green to

Poncirus trifoliata 'Flying Dragon'

purple-burgundy while *Ilex decidua*'s bright red berries show up better as its leaves fall. Frost glistens on the field in the morning light. The maples retain some yellow leaves but the higher ones have fallen. This is the great transition. From a low near freezing we went to sixty degrees and I went from lined to unlined jeans.

In mid-November we celebrated Cathy's birthday. Brie and Cheryl produced salads and pirogi and I made a cake. Ippy joined us and we laughed and talked while we ate. We picked up a few acorns, dug out a few aggressive salvias, and potted on very few plants. It was a day of rejoicing.

We continued refining the Blue and Yellow Garden. We cleared away plants that intruded into the path and removed salvias near the boxwoods. From the top of a ladder we finished cutting away the lowest branches on the rain tree, *Koelreuteria bipinnata*, and now can walk under it without bowing. We eliminated large sections of *Macleaya cordata*, plume poppy, a mass at the northeast corner that separates garden, wall, and barnyard. I first saw this plant at my mother-in-law's garden in Canada, where it grew at the corner of a terrace. Its gray-blue leaves and plumes of pinkish beige flowers were the perfect ending to the bed. She warned me of its aggressive nature but assured me it could be easily controlled. I bought a plant shortly after we moved here and remove about half of the mass each fall, spreading compost over the cleared area.

When Craufurd comes home early from the university at this season, he resumes his Sisyphean task of removing the beaver dam in the spillway at the pond. Craufurd and the beaver work equally hard at their tasks. No sooner does the beaver build his dam — and a major dam it is with logs, sticks, and mud — than Craufurd comes along with rake, hoe, mattock, and whatever else he needs to tear it down. This is a serious clash of wills. If the beaver builds his dam higher than ours, the water will wash away our dam and the pond will disappear down the Eno River. The problem arises because the beaver has little else to do while Craufurd has classes to teach, books to write, community activities in which to participate, and, at this moment, the department of economics at Duke University to chair.

We began our annual revision of the Tropical Garden, originally called the Purple and Orange Border, which, from the beginning, was a misnomer. Some orange flowers grow here but most are golden yellow, vivid magenta, or scarlet. The foliage is green, chartreuse, or burgundy. True purple, that is, half blue and half red, doesn't really work in this area. This garden combines flowers in fully saturated colors with bold, lush foliage.

This space contained a formal rose garden, invaded by Bermuda grass, when we moved to Montrose. A trellis that supported boysenberries divided the area into two sections. I weeded the roses that first spring, digging out the grass with a garden fork. After Wayne built the lath house, we removed the trellis and Craufurd began to improve the soil. He grew crop after crop of buckwheat, tilling it under each time it bloomed. We planted the new garden in the summer of 1989 and it was a primary feature of our first Garden Seminar in 1990. We laid out a drip irrigation system that was cut into inadvertently with a shovel and destroyed the first year. About that time I concluded that the only responsible approach to perennial droughts was careful preparation of the soil and mulch rather than pouring water on desiccated plants. I haven't missed the irrigation at all. Today, as I dug out cannas, I removed the last bits of plastic pipe from that failed experiment.

We cut down bananas and mulched their roots with about two feet of shredded leaves. We thinned the cannas, digging deeply to remove their rhizomatous roots and to incorporate the remains of last summer's mulch. We carried every bit of organic matter without a tuber, bulb, or seed to the compost pile, put the rest on the brush pile, and spread the remnants of last fall's leaves, now partly decomposed, over the ground. I am glad we have four seasons. This garden provides a feeling of enclosure at its peak in early fall but now that we have cleared off the beds and can see across all the

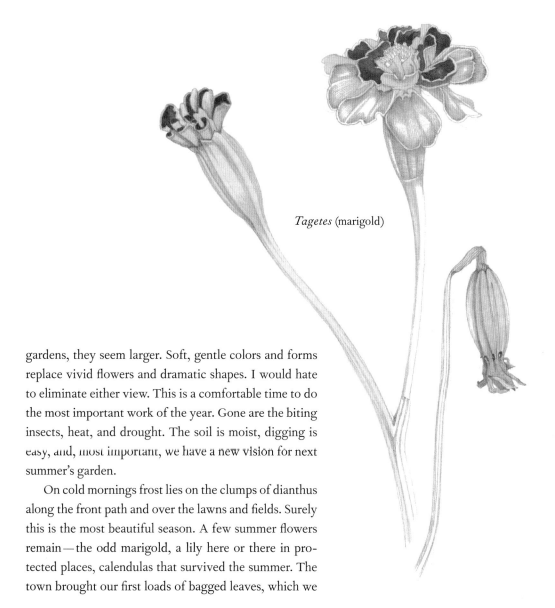

Tagetes (marigold)

gardens, they seem larger. Soft, gentle colors and forms replace vivid flowers and dramatic shapes. I would hate to eliminate either view. This is a comfortable time to do the most important work of the year. Gone are the biting insects, heat, and drought. The soil is moist, digging is easy, and, most important, we have a new vision for next summer's garden.

On cold mornings frost lies on the clumps of dianthus along the front path and over the lawns and fields. Surely this is the most beautiful season. A few summer flowers remain—the odd marigold, a lily here or there in pro-tected places, calendulas that survived the summer. The town brought our first loads of bagged leaves, which we

hauled to the compost bins where we alternated a layer of leaves with a layer of partly decomposed compost. After six layers we were warm. By the end of the month the garden had regained its wintry character. Leaves have fallen from the deciduous hollies, *Ilex decidua* 'Pocahontas', leaving their branches lined with clusters of brilliant red berries. Even the yellow-berried cultivar, *I. d.* 'Finch's Golden', has berries this year. Why this year and not last year? Perhaps we had a frost when the trees were in flower. Perhaps they can't support a heavy crop of berries every year. *Mahonia* x *wagneri* has burgundy leaves and *Helleborus multifidus* subsp. *hercegovinus*, near their base, has swollen, fat, green buds above ground. These vivid green hellebores intensify the purple mahonia leaves and the brilliant red berries on the hollies above them.

I began a new garden of snowdrops, *Galanthus elwesii* var. *monostictus*. My inspiration is a mental picture of a large wooded area with thousands of snowdrops in bloom every November. They would mark the change from fall to winter. The flowering stalk of this early-flowering variety grows up between two gray-green leaves, one of which emerges from within the other. The inner cup of the flower has shorter petals with only one elongated green mark on the outside of each petal and a large, lighter green mark inside. This new snowdrop garden, now the Snowdrop Woods, a large area in the Old Garden, will be visible from the south edge of the walk along the Aster Border. I can see it now from the lath house, because I know where to look and what to look for. It took the entire month to plant the Snowdrop Woods. Several tightly packed clumps, that must not have been divided since my original planting, produced hundreds of bulbs. I separated each bulb from its neighbors and planted them five or six inches apart. The entire time I planted I thought of how it will look in another year, five years, and, perhaps, twenty-five years from now. Someday there will be a carpet of snowdrops, and I may get to see them!

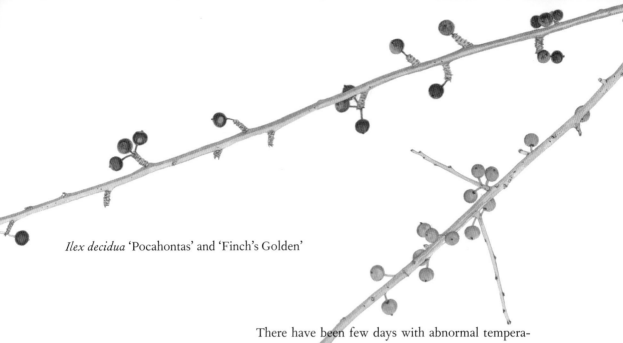

Ilex decidua 'Pocahontas' and 'Finch's Golden'

There have been few days with abnormal temperatures. Rain that began in late August came just in time and all the creatures and plants soaked it up for a grand finale. This is the best fall ever. A few leaves remain on oaks, bowdocks (*Maclura pomifera*), young beeches, maples, and some deciduous shrubs but most trees are bare and we can see all the way across the flood plain. Buds beneath the chartreuse yellow leaves on *Chimonanthus praecox* are swollen, ready to open. *Osmanthus heterophyllus* blooms with clusters of tiny white flowers that perfume the west side of the garden near the house. When I work in the woods I am seldom alone. I hear the noise of other creatures as they walk or scurry through crisp, fallen leaves. I can distinguish the sound of heavy, plodding human feet from those of running animals.

One member of the staff came in late with one eye almost completely closed. She must have rubbed her eyes after weeding and had poison ivy on top of one eyelid and under another. Again I felt the burden of responsibility. "Just call me and I will pull it up!" I shout. Fortunately, I am not allergic. I do not offer to remove hornets' nests nor beehives, nor to carry every heavy load, and I cannot do much about heat or cold. The little heater in the potting room keeps that building fairly warm in winter and a few cold towels cool the staff in summer.

Thanksgiving came and went without my spending the day in the kitchen. I weeded the little garden between the sunny gardens and woods. This section has no name, primarily because I am usually the person who weeds it, and I never have to tell anyone to go there. The naming of gardens is not a whimsical thing. If I needed to tell someone to go to the area where nandinas grow, I would have to describe the route. "Walk north along the driveway past the deciduous holly, *Ilex verticillata*, to the area planted with *Helleborus foetidus*, and a curving mass of nandinas." I prefer "Go to Nandinaland."

We worked on the Basin, the newly named area from which we moved a brush pile last March. We weeded and mulched the flat land and bank and lined the path with juniper logs. I have thought about plants suitable for that soil and for part sun ever since we cleared it last year, and I've settled on *Iris tectorum*, the Japanese rooftop iris, along the banks, and an ophiopogon with slender blades and tight growth as a ground cover for the flat areas. Later this fall we will divide colchicums and interplant them with mondo grass and in future years will see flowers from the lawn above. That is simpler than taking visitors into the woods, which, in early fall, can be a haven for mosquitoes.

We weeded out grasses and little maples in the grove of junipers and redbuds adjacent to the Basin where *Rhapidophyllum hystrix*, needle palm, grows in the dense shade beneath these trees. We mulched the area deeply in preparation for a cover crop of rohdeas, which will eventually form a carpet of deep green, strap-like leaves and bright red berries in winter. This year we don't just talk about plans for the future. We realize them largely because of the competent, cooperative staff, full of energy and enthusiasm. At times like this I believe I will complete the woods garden all the way to the broad plateau from which we see the flood plain.

We rescued a shrew from Roger's soft mouth. At first glance I couldn't tell whether it was a vole or a shrew, but if the latter, it did not need taming. Someone held it for Ippy to draw, then set it down to return to its home in the mulch. As we gathered acorns, roots and all, in the Circle Garden, we saw what appeared to be plastic flowers. They (rounded earthstars) looked like silvery gray stars with extra points and a chocolate kiss in the middle. As Ippy drew one in the heat of the building where she works, the chocolate part puffed up, the points curved under, and when she touched the top, puffs of spores came out.

We go to London the first week in December and I grow increasingly anxious about it. The staff will take care of the garden, cats, and greenhouses, and they are all completely reliable and trustworthy, but something unexpected always happens. A cat doesn't feel well. A new pest appears on a plant. We receive more leaves than we can spread in a lifetime. A torrential rain floods the basement and greenhouse. A windstorm topples a tree and we lose power. These are just a few of the potential problems that may arise. When Craufurd travels, he simply leaves and I assume his responsibilities. If we both go away, I must find people to take over all of our duties and teach them the eccentricities of the place. He thinks it is important for me to leave occasionally and I know he is right. But I am tied to this place in every way. The main problem for me is that I don't mind it. I have created a complex paradise and am reluctant to miss a day in it, much less a week.

DECEMBER

A major winter storm is forecast for Piedmont North Carolina. A cold front coming south from Canada will collide with a large low pressure system going north from the Gulf. Although we hope for either rain or snow, we fear freezing rain, wind, and sleet. We lowered the slatted shades on the greenhouses to protect the glass panels in case we get ice or snow that will fall in large, heavy chunks when it melts. As the day approaches we hear dire predictions for the storm, now expected to arrive at noon on the day we leave, continue for a day, and deposit half an inch to an inch of snow and ice. Power outages will be common.

Snow began at noon as predicted and every flake remained where it landed. We found people at the last minute to stay in the house and care for the cats. The van driver was thirty-five minutes late and by the time we left home, the ground, trees, and roads were covered with snow and the snow had changed to freezing rain. It took nearly three hours to reach the airport traveling between five and fifteen miles an hour. Visibility was terrible and the traffic was bumper to bumper with all lanes filled. Our driver could barely see out of the front windows, and not at all out of the side or back of the van. He played talk radio at high volume for his pleasure and our annoyance during the trip. We arrived at the airport thirty minutes before departure time and anxiously waited in line, hoping to get through the check-in process and security examinations before the gate for our flight closed. For the first time ever we rejoiced when we heard that the departure would be fifteen minutes later than scheduled.

The security attendant warned me that my shoes might set off the metal detectors, but I said I would take my chances. I had worn those shoes on other flights and didn't want to hold us up. That was the wrong decision. The shoes must have metal shafts, for they set off alarms which delayed both of us as I was frisked with hands and instruments and left to struggle back into my shoes. Time was short and I was nervous.

We boarded later than expected because the cleaning crew needed extra time to prepare the plane, and then the plane needed to be de-iced. I was happy to have them take as much time as necessary to do both. Shortly after we settled into our seats and heard the safety instructions, the pilot announced another forty-minute delay. I looked out the window and saw ice building up on the wings. He made announcements every forty minutes or so, always saying the same thing, "We are next in line to be de-iced and then we will be on our way." Flight attendants served orange juice, Sprite, and tiny packages of pretzels. They showed a full-length movie. Shortly after eleven o'clock the airport ran out of de-icing fluid, the flight was cancelled, and we were told there were only a few seats left for the same flight the next day. We raced our fellow passengers to the ticket counter, reserved seats for the next day, collected our bags, and hired a cab to drive us to Hillsborough. Our driver talked on his cell phone practically the entire time when I thought he should be clutching the steering wheel with both hands. Loud talk radio at night is something I hope never to hear again. We heard ads for dating services. "We can introduce you to someone who is as interesting as you are. We can help you find the happiness you deserve." Salt and fewer cars made the roads safer than they had been earlier in the day. The sky lit up as we drove west from the airport. The driver said it was lightning from a thunderstorm. In fact it was trees falling onto power lines that collapsed and blew transformers. The road in front of Montrose was the worst; ice over snow made the hill nearly impassable.

When we reached home, we couldn't get into the house because we had decided at the last minute to lock our new, heavy storm doors and failed to add their keys to our rings. We rang the doorbell again and again and threw snow at the window of the guest room, finally waking the house sitters. We slept hard but not long. All night we heard breaking branches falling with terrible thuds onto the garden and lawns. I went to the window many times to see whether the great oak in the Rock Garden survived. Limb after limb of the deodara cedar, *Cedrus deodara*, fell in a heap at the edge of the porch and across the Dianthus Walk.

We woke to a house cooling down rapidly without power. Craufurd started the generator that could power the furnace, a few electric outlets, the refrigerator, and hot water, but not all at once. We had to turn off the refrigerator to make coffee and the furnace to heat water for baths. We ate peanut butter, cheese, and crackers for breakfast but we had fresh coffee. When we surveyed the damage around the house, we found large limbs lying at the base of nearly every tree. Many junipers, least able to withstand the weight of ice and snow, lost a third of their mass.

I have lived through other ice storms, devastating hurricanes, and a tornadic downdraft. I know the garden will recover even though it can never be the same. Scars will heal. New sprouts and branches will grow where others fell. We began the massive cleanup, clearing off the driveway first. Craufurd cut large branches into pieces small enough for us to carry to the brush piles. Next we began on the Metasequoia Garden, where juniper branches lay in heaps over the entire area. We cancelled our flight for that night and booked one for the next day.

I finally walked the property after lunch and found enormous branches fallen from the junipers throughout the garden. The firs managed their load of ice but the redbud at the northwest corner of the May Garden split into three giant pieces and lay across the bed. White pines in the front of the property looked as if their branches were clean-cut at the trunk and remained where they had fallen, neatly stacked one on top of the other. Fragile hackberries lost piles of branches and a large uprooted pine fell across the cyclamen in the Mother-in-Law Walk. By this time, almost no one in central North Carolina had any power. We ransacked the refrigerator and fixed an enormous salad of everything that was cooked or edible raw plus a tin of tuna

tossed with "Miracle-Gro," our euphemism for Miracle Whip. Exhausted physically and emotionally, I finally gave up and took a long nap.

We spent the next morning hauling debris until we could barely move. It was difficult to drag a cart laden with heavy branches over ice-covered ground and painful to watch people stomping around on the plants in the Metasequoia Garden. Trees still burdened with ice split and fell all day long. Duke Power made no promise of power, saying it would take at least four or five more days to repair the lines. Temperatures in the teens made me worry about the tropical plants in the greenhouses. Roger Haile photographed the deadly beauty shortly before we left again for London. The same van driver picked us up, even earlier than we had hoped he would two days before, and we arrived at the airport in forty minutes. This time I removed my shoes when we went through security checks. We settled down to read and write and tried to put Montrose, its condition, and the work ahead of us into the back of our minds. I bought snacks, in case we didn't get anything more than pretzels again. We boarded the plane on time and, as I sat with a sense of apprehension, I knew that I couldn't anticipate, dread, or prepare any further. We couldn't go back again.

After a comfortable flight of about six and a half hours, we landed in London. I thought back to my first air trip, which was to meet Craufurd's parents, in 1957. I remember the vibrations that went from the front to the back of the plane. The noise and my fear left me so exhausted I slept until about eleven the next morning. His family had eaten breakfast, and when Mr. Goodwin came in from the garden bearing a scythe with which he was cutting little saplings, he asked me to explain what was going on with our State Department. I had just taken my final exams at Duke and barely knew the name of the Secretary of State. I suddenly wished I could go home on the next noisy, rattling plane. It was less frightening.

We noticed many changes in London since our first visit more than forty years earlier. This time we found stores open on Sunday, supermarket-style grocery stores with central checkout counters instead of long, separate queues for meats, cheese, bread, etc. There was little heat in any building in the early 1960s. Our first flat had a tiny gas heater greedy for shillings and stingy with heat and I dressed in layers long before it became fashionable. This year we found every building we entered comfortably warm. Now the tube stations are clean with more elaborate and efficient entrances and exits. We were much younger when we first lived in London and always walked up or down the moving escalators, sometimes taking two steps at a time. Now we stand clutching the railings. In the early days we never thought about getting senior citizen discounts (concessions). For all I know, they didn't exist. Several years ago we began to request them. Now we are given them without comment. On buses and trains I was offered seats reserved for the elderly, handicapped, or women with infants. At first I refused, but quickly discovered that gray hair and wrinkles have some advantages and I accepted without a pause. I don't feel like an old person and can probably haul more mulch and turn more compost than most, but I do like a seat on a fast-moving train.

We visited museums, spent an evening with Tony and Frances Bradshaw, and a day in the research center at the Tate Britain. A dark and cold day with light showers and strong winds forced us to abandon the idea of visiting Kew Gardens. After five days we were ready to return to the many unfinished chores in Hillsborough. We knew the cats were fine; we had daily reports on them. But we worried about the house and garden.

Although the power was on when we reached home, and more limbs had fallen, it was a relief to find most trees still standing. The house hadn't suffered and my own bed felt wonderful. Heavy rain the first day back meant no staff, and I could catch up inside before continuing the cleanup outside. By the next day I was glad to begin on it and in three days Craufurd and I had cleared five areas completely.

First I cleared the debris from the Snowdrop Woods, knowing that if I had just one part of the garden as it would have been without the storm, I could sustain my optimism and clear the rest. New crocuses were there, ready to bloom, snowdrops had risen above ground, and a winter-flowering colchicum, *C. hungaricum*, showed buds about to open. We hauled away branches from our mature poplars, *Liriodendron tulipifera*. With ratchet pruners, we cut away enough of the smaller limbs to leave a log we could carry. Now I know how to find the point where weight is evenly distributed and can lift larger, heavier pieces than I did in the past. I handed large pieces of wood to someone on top of the brush pile and she threw them into the interior, which, before we started, had looked like a giant doughnut hole.

Each day we worked on a different section of the garden, rescuing plants in growth. We cleaned off the Metasequoia Garden, filling each cart with branches passed from person to person as if in a fire brigade. We rolled pieces of juniper twelve inches thick off plants and onto the path and at the end of the day uncovered the *Helleborus niger* I had seen in bloom just before the storm hit. The first flower was still there, nearly buried in juniper needles, but now three more stems bore buds about four inches above ground. Large clumps of snowdrops were intact and crocuses, *C. laevigatus* and *C. imperati*, had visible flower buds.

Craufurd cut the largest branches of juniper and hackberry into movable chunks and we finished cleaning up Jo's Bed. The old juniper at the corner is little more than a stick now, with tufts of needles sticking out here and there, but if it grows again in spring, we won't cut it down. Perhaps it will eventually provide the dense dark background needed in that corner of the bed. Paul Gove assures us he can repair the cast iron fence broken by falling branches.

On the shortest day of the year, December 21, the sun rose at 7:22 and set at 5:05, and I worked outside until nearly six, when dim light finally forced me inside. On the next day I had an extra minute; the sun set at 5:06. I knew how to spend it!

The garden, though bruised, is more attractive with the fluff of last summer removed. Edges have reappeared on the straight paths through the sunny gardens. We see the beauty of the urns without their distracting summer plants. Trees without leaves reveal their skeletal shapes. The pair of persimmons near our little nursery have craggy, deeply indented bark on dark gray trunks and angular branches, and the metasequoias without their needles reveal next year's flowering stalks that will elongate as winter

Helleborus niger

approaches spring. Although the foliage of blackberry lilies, *Belamcanda chinensis*, looks tired, the clusters of ripe fruit still look like blackberries.

I can't do Christmas this year. Each day the branches lie on the garden I fear I will lose something else. In areas where the limbs lie thickly, no light penetrates to the plants below. This garden is my obsession and my delight. I won't miss the joy of Christmas if it is replaced by the sight of one more garden uncovered.

Cold rain kept me inside. I cleaned the house and made a few preparations for Christmas. When Craufurd and I bought our first house forty years ago, I decided to do my housework on rainy days and spend the remainder of my time teaching, playing music, or working in the garden. This schedule was doomed to failure from the beginning. The garden looked good and I was intrigued by every aspect of it. I played better than ever and taught with enthusiasm, but the house—well, any house needs regular attention. Now I have a schedule for all household chores, and the best times of my life—those spent in the garden—are dictated by weather, the season, and the challenge of the moment. No two days are the same.

Christmas day was cold, clear, and sunny, but extremely windy. As the winds strengthened, more damaged branches fell. Craufurd and I had a quiet morning together and I spent the afternoon making my annual flower count. I anticipate this event for days and hope Christmas Eve won't be so cold that the flowers open then will be too damaged to count the next day. The weather cooperated and I saw the following: *Iris unguicularis* 'Walter Butt' and a medium purple-flowered seedling; *Phlox subulata* with flowers in lilac, blue, and pink; white *Verbena canadensis*; *Erica* x *darleyensis* 'Furzey' and 'Arthur Johnson'; *Crocus speciosus* and *C. laevigatus*; *Osmanthus heterophyllus*; *Viburnum tinus* and *V. macrocephalum*; *Cyclamen coum*; *Helleborus niger*, *H. cyclophyllus*, *H. argutifolius*, *H. foetidus*; *Jasminum nudiflorum*; *Mahonia* x *media* 'Winter Sun'; *Clematis cirrhosa*; *Narcissus romieuxii*; *Galanthus elwesii* var. *monostictus* and *G. transcaucasicus*; *Isopyrum biternatum*; *Spiraea*

Belamcanda chinensis

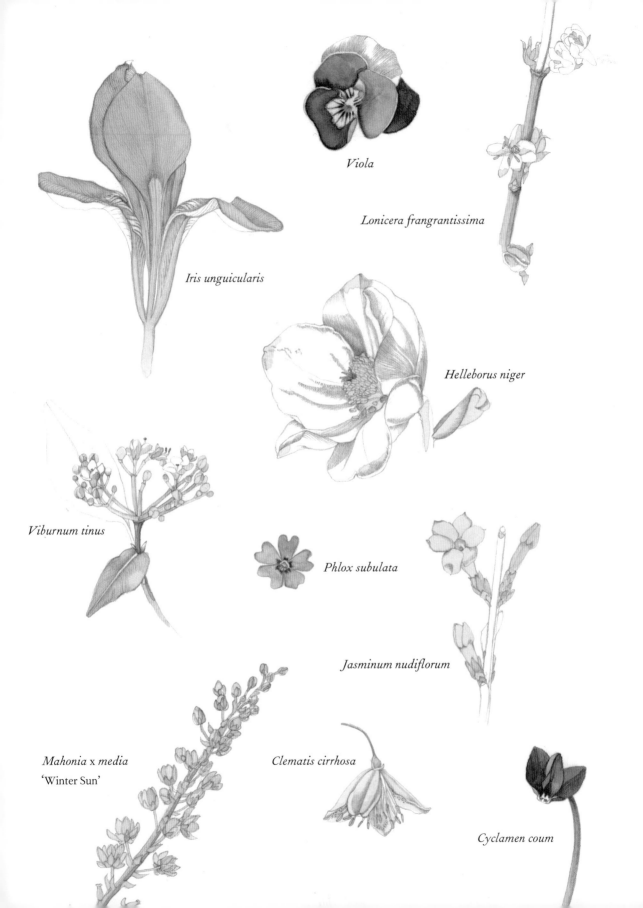

Viola

Lonicera frangrantissima

Iris unguicularis

Helleborus niger

Viburnum tinus

Phlox subulata

Jasminum nudiflorum

Mahonia x *media*
'Winter Sun'

Clematis cirrhosa

Cyclamen coum

prunifolia; *Erinus alpinus*; *Lonicera fragrantissima*; *Chae-nomeles* x *superba* 'Crimson and Gold'; *Lamium macula-tum* white; *Aster carolinianus*; *Viola cornuta* blue; *Primula vulgaris*; *Colchicum hungaricum*; and a dandelion, *Taraxa-cum officinale*. This list makes the garden sound as if it was in full bloom, but many plants had only one flower. I didn't cheat. I saw stamens on at least one bloom of each species.

We live at the top of a small hill. The land slopes away from the house on all sides. Terraces throughout much of the property prevent erosion but the angle of the slope determines how much protection we have during storms. In general the areas facing south and east are barely touched by damaging winds while those facing west bear the brunt of every storm. I pulled branches from those sections in the woods garden where there is major damage and carried away many logs from the fallen pine in the Mother-in-Law Walk. Some plants seem fated to have a difficult life in my garden. A man drove his bobcat over *Helleborus multifidus* subsp. *istriacus* six years ago. He drove through the woods garden, over trilliums, this

Aster carolinianus

special hellebore, and everything else between the lawn and the stump of a large white oak, *Quercus alba*, that he erroneously thought he could set upright after Hurricane Fran uprooted it. Miraculously, both hellebore and trilliums bloomed the following spring. When it fell, the pine tree pulled this same, tortured hellebore out of the ground, so I replanted it in the hope it will recover again.

At ground level the garden begins to look as it did before the storm, but if we look up, we see great scars on almost every tree. Poplars have bright creamy white gashes, while the junipers are deep burgundy red surrounded by beige, and maples have reddish-orange centers surrounded by cream. The brilliant colors of the interiors of the damaged trees are beginning to fade, but the jagged tears left as the weight of ice and snow tore limbs from tree trunks will remain until we bring in an arborist to trim the stubs close to the trunks. We can't do that until the ground hardens in summer.

A week past the shortest day doesn't give us much more daylight. Light arrives two minutes later, at 7:24 in the morning, and leaves five minutes later, at 5:09 in the evening. It doesn't add much time for gardening. Craufurd and I spent the last few evenings in the year shelling the few pecans that ripened this year. We must wait at least twelve more months for our next good crop.

The entire staff will return to work in early January. It will be good to get back to a normal schedule. Four people working together can accomplish an enormous amount. I enjoyed my break and my solitude, but prefer our regular routine.

JANUARY

Rain and the first week of the year confined me to the law office, where I dealt with the "year in numbers," as Ippy calls it. I began to prepare W-2s for my staff and final tax forms for federal and state governments. I, a computer illiterate, created a program in the hope that I could eliminate mathematical errors but it took more than six hours to reconcile a $2.90 discrepancy.

When I got outside to clear the leaves off the Rock Garden, I had first to remove a large, newly fallen oak limb, damaged by the ice and brought down with the rain. Then I knelt and, using my hands as gentle rakes, pulled away the oak leaves. I am late this year, for the oak held onto its leaves until after the storm and I see little advantage to clearing off just a few leaves. When all have fallen, we remove them first from the Circle Garden on the west side of the Rock Garden. Most of our wind comes from the west and will blow leaves in neighboring beds onto the Rock Garden as quickly as we clear them off. I looked for treasures as I cleared rock crevices and pulled out chickweed, wild onions, and cress with bare fingers. *Crocuses laevigatus* and *sieberi* were in bud; *Cyclamen coum* had flowers nearly open; and the gray-green leaves and white buds of *Galanthus elwesii* were well above the soil. Stiff but fragile gray-green spears of *Iris reticulata* were at least an inch high. Fat buds of *Adonis amurensis* had risen above ground; worried that each step might crush an emerging shoot of some winter flowering bulb, I circled around them, removing leaves above and below the clumps.

Cheryl found *Tecophilaea cyanocrocus* trying to bloom in the little greenhouse. Its brilliant blue flower was stuck between the leaves. With slender tweezers I gently pulled apart the inhibiting leaves and within a few hours the flower opened and Ippy drew it. I was excited about this plant when I first saw it last winter, but it is even more exciting now, for we brought it through

Tecophilaea cyanocrocus

a summer and back into flower a second year. After the foliage died away last spring, I set the pot under a bench in the greenhouse, where it received no water until we repotted it in late summer. This, the Chilean crocus, has special meaning for Ippy, for she grew up in Chile, and it was the first plant she drew for this book recording a year at Montrose.

The first week of January was filled with celebrations. On Tuesday we had a party, which was a major surprise because it wasn't anyone's birthday. On Friday we went to Cathy's farm in Person County. She lives part of her life in a round house that she and her husband, Jim, built in a community of friends who share 160 acres of open space. The Dykes also own the adjacent hundred acres of woodlands, ponds, and fields. Brie, Cheryl, Ippy, and I walked with Cathy over much of it, going slowly, examining the ground as we walked. We saw brilliant chartreuse mosses that looked like the finest silk velvet and lichens in shades of gray, olive-green, red, and orange. Ippy wanted to crawl into an enormous hollow tree lying where it fell to learn what it felt like to be a tree. Cheryl found an interesting stone we believe to be a Native American grinding tool. Gingers (*Asarum arifolium*) with gray or purple leaves mottled with gray and silver and ground cedar (*Lycopodium complanatum*) grow near Christmas ferns (*Polystichum acrostichoides*) all through the woods. The cover of beeches keeps the undergrowth down and we walked easily from place to place. We returned to the house for a delicious lunch of sweet potato soup, Ippy's grandmother's focaccia, and a grand-looking dark chocolate cake. The week ended at Ippy's and Neil's for dinner on Saturday where dessert was a caramel mousse similar to the pies mother used to make for my birthday. It was the perfect end to a birthday week.

We spread many bags of leaves beneath the weeping cherries below the old dry stone wall south of the sunny gardens and transplanted nearly one thousand *Rohdea japonica* seedlings in the area beneath the junipers near the basin. Rohdeas, drought-tolerant plants, will eventually grow together and form a solid, weed-inhibiting mass. The contrast of somber, green needles of the junipers above and shining, medium green leaves of rohdeas beneath will transform this dull area into an interesting one. Some of these seedlings sown in 1997 and 1998 will have their first clusters of red berries by next winter.

By the second week of January we had returned to our normal routine. Cheryl sowed seeds of tender spring annuals; Cathy stuck cuttings of conifers; Brie planted divisions of special narcissus in the Basin; and I removed more oak leaves and germinated acorns from the Rock Garden. We fertilized all actively growing bulbs in both greenhouses and pulled up several thousand little maple seedlings from the woods. I continued planting the new Snowdrop Woods with other forms of snowdrops divided from thick clumps throughout the garden.

Cold air and no sun prompted us to close the cold frames early. I worked in the law office until I felt sleepy and went to bed early. At one o'clock in the morning I heard the wind roar and remembered we had not secured the cold frame covers with bungee cords. I comforted myself with the knowledge that the covers would most likely stay in place, and even if they blew off, the wooden sides of each frame provide some protection. I turned over and tried to go back to sleep but the wind continued without a pause and I finally gave in and put on my warmest socks, real shoes (not bedroom slippers), my heaviest coat over my pajamas, and a warm hat. With a Coleman lantern to light the way I went down to the cold frames below the big greenhouse. Four covers had blown off and there was ice on the others still in place. I replaced the covers, fastened all of them with cords, and returned to the house. The sky was so clear I saw thousands of stars and the cold air so invigorating I returned to bed wide awake and read Beth Chatto's *Woodland Garden* until sleep finally came an hour later.

Even though the temperature reached only forty-two degrees the next day, we all worked outside for at least part of the time clearing oak leaves off the Scree Garden and removing magnolia leaves from arums and hellebores. We potted up the lesser celandine (*Ranunculus ficaria* 'Brazen Hussy'), a special blue-flowered dwarf crested iris (*Iris cristata*), and green-and-gold (*Chrysogonum virginianum*). I continued weeding and clearing the leaves off the east side of the Rock Garden, and we sprayed the entire garden with our homemade deer repellent.

We cut away about 90 percent of the old growth and rewove the remaining canes on *Rosa wichurana* 'Curiosity'. We will control it by winding the new shoots around and around the post. If they grow up, we will bring them down into the mass. If they grow out to the side we will poke them back into the framework of branches. At this moment *R. w.* 'Curiosity' looks like a few, skimpy sticks pulled together around a post, but by spring fresh new leaves and shoots will give this rose a relaxed, more comfortable shape. And if they don't, we will dig it out.

After two warm days it was a relief to return to winter. Normal temperatures are best. Unseasonably warm weather, no matter how comfortable, lures plants into flower and growth, and that often leads to major losses. *Iris unguicularis* was blooming as it should in the Circle Garden, and in the beds around the house, masses of snowdrops had risen above ground, and the dark green tips of crocuses were visible nearby. I rejoice in this season.

Craufurd and I spent most of a weekend indoors. I feel a slight unease if I don't work outside for at least part of each day. One day doesn't make

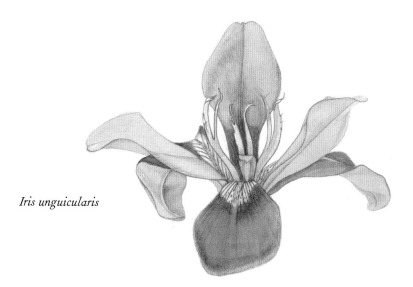

Iris unguicularis

much difference. Two days means a fretful sleep and three days leaves me unable to concentrate on anything except music. Sunday afternoon I escaped into the garden and built several little log fences around vulnerable young shrubs. First I made a triangle or square of short juniper (cedar) logs on the ground, then crossed those with a second triangle, and sometimes placed a third layer of logs above those. Perhaps this will deter our head-rubbing deer.

By the end of the second week in January, promises filled the winter landscape. Hellebores showed their young flower stalks in the woodland gardens. Winter aconites had collars of green and round, bright yellow buds ready to open with the first touch of the sun, and the first shoots of *Galanthus nivalis*, planted a year ago, appeared in the Snowdrop Walk. *Cyclamen coum* and *C. pseudibericum* bloomed beneath the deodara cedar in the front lawn and *Chimonanthus praecox* perfumed the air. *Crocus imperati* subsp. *imperati* opened beige buds

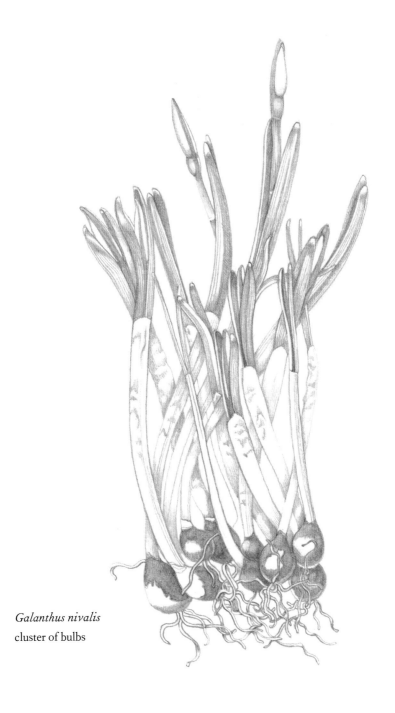

Galanthus nivalis
cluster of bulbs

striped with purple to reveal fragrant, violet interiors and *C. sieberi* 'Albus' opened white ones with bright yellow bases near *Helleborus niger* by the driveway. In the greenhouse, *Tecophilaea cyanocrocus* sent up a second flower bud and small narcissus species showed buds or flowers.

Another winter storm was predicted for mid-January. This time the forecasters said we would have snow and that it would not be a major weather event, but I worried. We hadn't finished cleaning up the woods and lawns from the December storm, had barely begun our usual winter chores, and felt we couldn't spend two more weeks hauling sticks. With many plants in growth or flower, a major storm now would do even more damage to the garden than the one in December. About an inch and a half of snow fell—just enough to close schools and disrupt much of the activity in town. Grocery store shelves were empty by the night before. White fluffy frosting on plants in the Circle Garden gave it a different shape and morning was silent without the noisy, diesel engines of school buses or announcements over the loudspeakers next door.

Days and nights remained cold, with temperatures in the upper thirties and low-to-mid-forties, but we were comfortable in vests over layers of shirts. Each day brought forth more flowers on cyclamen, snowdrops, and crocuses. Robins ate the berries on the holly near the driveway, and bluebirds sang their gurgling songs all day. We had exactly ten hours of daylight and I worked outside for about eight of them.

Cheryl pruned the wounded shrubs in Jo's Bed, cutting out branches that crossed their neighbors, damaged

Chimonanthus praecox

ones, and those that stuck out in all directions. When she finished, we had elegant plants that didn't look like they had been pummeled with ice-coated branches. Light and air reached their interiors and, best of all, they looked as if they just grew that way.

I reduced the enormous clump of *Saccharum arundinaceum*, a massive grass related to sugar cane. Last winter we left it intact in the Blue and Yellow Garden until early spring, but this year the ice storm had broken the stalks and the plant looked ragged. First we cut the grass down to about a foot above ground, then Brie, Cathy, and Cheryl left to work in other areas. I dug with my favorite transplant spade (the one with a long, curved blade), then with my best digging fork, and finally with a mattock. Working from the outside, I chopped away several inches at a time. When I reached the woody center, I saw new roots about fifteen inches above ground. They weren't even touching soil. I removed nearly two-thirds of the plant, added compost mixed with soil around the base, and mulched the area around it. Next year I must dig out the remains and plant them deeper.

In 1985 I convinced Craufurd to cut some of the walnuts and other large trees in the main path below the upper slope in the woods. Mr. Paschall, our arborist from Durham—we called him a tree man then—and his sons cut the trees. We had the larger walnut trees cut into boards, cured them for several years, and had them made into a bookcase, shutters, steps, and a table. The Paschalls threw the smaller logs into a sunken area near the big rocks in the woods. Along with the walnut, they put bowdock and sweet gum logs into the area.

We began to remove this unsightly pile in mid-January. Much of the walnut and bowdock was just as hard when it came out as when it went in more than fifteen years ago. We dug out blackberries, smilax (the horrid one with thorns all along each stem and large tuberous roots), poison ivy, honeysuckle, and verbesina. We uncovered elaborate woodchuck tunnels and

hope our disruption drives them away. We found and left a few self-sown rohdeas, *Rohdea japonica*, and Christmas ferns, *Polystichum acrostichoides*, at the base of the woodpile. Cally and Roger stayed with us as we worked. Roger sat in the sun while Cally ran circles around him. From time to time the little gray cat stood sideways, arched his back, and puffed out his fur, making himself look as large as possible. That sent the dog running the other way around the circle. There was no hissing, no growling. They declared an end to the game or perhaps time out by rubbing noses. At first I didn't know what to plant in this newly reclaimed area but knew I would study it when standing in front of it and think of possibilities when lying in bed. This new garden must link the slope of rhododendrons and mountain laurels to its west with the large hellebore plantings to the east.

We walked over to Burnside to hear a concert. Burnside, Maureen Quilligan's and Michael Malone's home, is almost adjacent to Montrose. In the nineteenth century the properties were side by side, but Cameron Park School was built on part of their property about fifty years ago. The Bagg family, from Durham, performed trios and solos with violin, viola, and piano. Sam, age fifteen, played the piano I had sold to Michael, and at the conclusion of his performance of Chopin's Etude in F Major, op. 10, no. 8, I was overwhelmed. I had finally heard my piano as it was meant to be played, and by a young person with a lifetime of music ahead of him. I felt good about giving up the instrument. When I congratulated Sam on his sensitive performance, I discovered that the Baggs had purchased my "teaching" piano, a Mason & Hamlin grand I taught on in the law office twenty years earlier.

This is the coldest winter in about seven years—much colder than last winter. The water froze and a pipe burst at the east end of the big greenhouse. We had to wait a week before the ground thawed and we could finish demolishing the brush pile. After we dug and dragged the last partly decayed logs from above and below the surface of the ground, we spread loads of bagged leaves over the area. With great excitement Cathy and I brought over four stones covered with moss to form the bottom steps for the new garden. It didn't take long to decide how to develop the area. I had dreamed of a garden of planted steps for eleven years and finally had the perfect place—a semi-circular basin, sloping south. We will lay stones in an arc at intervals going up the slope and plant the flat areas between each step with cyclamen, crocuses, snowdrops, aconites, and early-flowering narcissus species. It will be a winter garden. The slope above the steps will be stabilized with mass plantings of several cultivars of *Acorus gramineus*, carex, ferns, and mahonias.

By the end of the month the threat of more snow and bitterly cold temperatures led us to further winterize the big greenhouse. We partially filled many plastic bags with leaves; set them against the doors, coolers, and water pipes; turned off the water outside; and drained the pipes. More bags of leaves went between pots of woody plants in the uncovered shallow cold

frames. Four inches of snow fell and no one came to work. It lay about for most of a week and remained even longer on the shady slopes in the woods, at the front door, and along the front walk. I had my winter's rest.

Cindy and Impy died late in January. Cindy went first on January 18. After working most of the day in the law office, I returned to the house at about three o'clock and found her facedown in her litter box. I wiped off her mouth, and sat and held her for over an hour. Although she made few

Winter flowers (crocuses, galanthus, winter aconites)

sounds, she grasped me as she lay against my arms. I wrapped a towel around her and laid her on her side so I could hold her front paws which by then had begun to get cold. She made tiny kneading motions. Finally I set her in a low box with the towel and peacefully she stopped breathing. Impy died ten days later. When I went into the house late one night, I found her lying on the steps. I held her and rubbed her, then watched while she climbed up and down the little stairs to the counter. She sat with her head over her water dish but didn't drink. When I rubbed water on her lips, she made no effort to lick it. She died during the night. I thought back to the happy day in 1984 when the kittens were born in Craufurd's study. Flossie, their mother, was fiercely protective and terrified our other cats, and when she died the winter after their birth, we kept all four kittens. Cindy, a gray tabby with a golden yellow star on her forehead, would sit on the back of my chair when I typed the acknowledgments for plant orders. She often lay on the table where we wrapped plants for shipping and often nibbled their leaves before we put them into boxes. She pranced with high steps and often led the way as I took groups of visitors through the garden.

Impy was a remarkably affectionate, gray tabby, always in motion even when she was a tiny kitten. When I opened the door to Craufurd's study, she would run to me, dash about the room where I sat, and collapse into a deep sleep in my lap. She followed us on long walks through the garden and woods and often crossed the spillway with me to explore our land on the east side of the pond. She was serious and small; most people thought she was a kitten, even at age eighteen.

We buried both cats in our cat cemetery at the north end of the May Garden. In many ways the death of the last of Flossie's kittens marks the end of the beginning. When they were born, I was struggling to find a solution to the conflicts in my life. I wanted to be outside working in my garden. I began Montrose Nursery that year and the kittens were a constant comfort to me during stressful times. Cats seem to understand such needs. We developed much of the garden during their eighteen-year lives.

I began this record a year ago. How do you end a circle? Some flowers have already appeared ahead of schedule, others will be late. This is little more than a summary of a cycle of seasons with no clear ending or beginning but overlapping expectations and hopes, disappointments and disillusions, surprises and rewards. The year was punctuated by small events—the first or last flower of a species, garden activities, weather, and special days. No two days were the same nor is the garden what it was a year ago or will be next year. The terrible heat and drought of summer killed some plants and weakened others. December's ice storm changed the pattern of light; now we have sun where before we had shade. Many small plants and single bulbs grew into clumps. We discovered in a painful way which tropical plants can withstand five days of subfreezing temperatures. We extended the garden farther into the woods and refined the Color Gardens. Most important, we expanded our vision and took a leap forward to enable the garden to survive beyond our lifetimes. The real story of this year is the deepening friendships of those who share the work and pleasure in managing the growth of the garden. We realize we will never finish this job. It is the doing of it that gives pleasure — the daily tasks, visions, and discoveries. Ippy brought a new dimension to our group as she illustrated the garden honestly, without embellishment. She brightened our days. Craufurd, my best friend, encouraged us. We celebrated when he approved of our efforts. This year, the happiest year of my life, is a tiny part of the story of Montrose.

INDEX

Page numbers in italic refer to illustrations

NANCY GOODWIN has written for *Fine Gardening*, *American Gardener*, *Horticulture*, *Veranda*, Country Home Country Gardens, and other magazines. She is a coauthor of *A Year in Our Gardens: Letters by Nancy Goodwin and Allen Lacy* and coeditor of *A Rock Garden in the South* by Elizabeth Lawrence. From 1984 to 1993, she operated Montrose Nursery, which specialized in unusual perennials such as hellebores and cyclamen.

IPPY PATTERSON has illustrated garden columns for the *New York Times*, the *Hartford Courant*, *McCall's Magazine*, and *Country Living Gardener Magazine*. She has illustrated numerous books, including *An Elizabethan Bestiary Retold*, *100 Flowers and How They Got Their Names*, and *No Bones*, for which she won the National Academy of Sciences Illustration Award in 1990.

Illustrator's note: I did these plant drawings on smooth paper with a hard pencil. The scenes of gardens, buildings, and animals I drew on a rougher paper with a softer pencil. I used watercolor pigment for the most part, but sometimes luma dyes, which are brighter, and only rarely a color pencil.

For the past thirty years I've used a .13 millimeter pen for drawings of this sort, but for this book I wanted to use pencil rather than ink because pencil lines convey softer, warmer, more lifelike forms than I can produce in ink. Happily, today's computer technology now allows clearer reproduction of this soft line than was possible in the past.

My rather casual use of color may seem arbitrary, but I did not want to obscure the penciled delineation. I was not attempting the realism of the traditional botanical illustrator. There are only a few hours in which to draw a single flower. The tissue of petals changes in front of one's eyes, and in the course of an afternoon's drawing, the sun moves in the sky and the stem and position of a flower move accordingly. All but two of these drawings were done from life; Tony and Beany were drawn from photographs. I sat or knelt on the ground for the rarest flowers. I valued these perspectives because they were closest to those that Nancy experiences hour upon hour from dawn to dusk, but I never felt I could do more than an impressionistic sketch this way. Cuttings and greenhouse or cold-frame plants were more accommodating models on my desk at Montrose or at my home studio.

Helleborus niger

LIBRARY OF CONGRESS

CATALOGING-IN-PUBLICATION DATA

Goodwin, Nancy (Nancy Sanders)
Montrose : life in a garden / Nancy Goodwin ;
with illustrations by Ippy Patterson ;
foreword by Maureen Quilligan.
p. cm.
Includes index.
ISBN 0-8223-3604-9 (cloth : alk. paper)
1. Montrose Garden (Hillsborough, N.C.) 2. Gardening–
North Carolina–Hillsborough. I. Title. SB466.U6G66 2005
712'.6'09756565–dc22
2005011387